W9-ATK-898

OTHER BOOKS AVAILABLE

I

STILL

Just Want to Pee Alone

collection of essays by

Some More Kick Ass Bloggers

TABLE OF CONTENTS

INTRODUCTION

Parenting is hard! Remember those commercials for the Peace Corps where they'd say it's "the toughest job you'll ever love?" Yeah, I don't think those people were ever parents. I mean, I haven't been in the Peace Corps, but there are many days where parenting seems a lot harder than digging wells in third world countries. O.K., being up to your waist in mud *does* sound miserable, but have you ever been up to your elbows in poop and then had your nose itch? *That* is pretty miserable too.

I've had many jobs in my life—no, digging wells was never one of them, but I did have to pick up my employer's dirty underwear from behind the bathroom door once. I've had many jobs in my life and parenting is one of the hardest. Think about it. Your hours are the worst, your boss is a tyrant, the pay sucks, you must work all holidays, and TGIF doesn't mean a thing to you.

Motherhood can be a hard and lonely job and if you can't laugh at yourself and your family, you're going to cry, so you might as well laugh.

This book is to let you know that you're not alone. We're not laughing at you, we're laughing with you.

Jen Mann
People I Want to Punch in the Throat

The Interview
By Amy Flory
Funny Is Family

I shift nervously in the waiting room chair, discreetly checking my pits for the moisture that is my constant companion in stressful situations. They're still dry, for now. The magazines in the waiting room aren't holding my attention, and as I wait for my job interview, my mind wanders. *Do I even want this job?* I ask myself for the hundredth time. *The hours are horrible, and the pay is even worse.*

Motherhood.

I know people who do this job. They seem to like it, and those broads are *always* recruiting.

"You'll love it!" they say.

"You'd be so good at it!" they encourage.

"It'll change your life!" they promise.

But that's the thing. I like my life. I don't think it needs to change. I'm good at my job and I make more money than the zero dollars per hour that motherhood boasts.

Yet, here I am. Drawn to the idea of this new path, compelled almost, I sit on an uncomfortable chair waiting to see if the hiring committee is going to see me as a welcome addition to the club.

"Amy Flory?" A brunette woman with glasses on her nose and spit-up on her shoulder peeks her head out of an office door and smiles.

I follow her in and take a seat at the table with the woman and two of her coworkers, all three of them with pads and pens in front of them, ready to take notes.

I mentally prepare my list of strengths, ready to insert them into every question I can.

1. I love to read, and if I've learned anything from watching television, most of parenting is reading to kids.
2. I've spent eight years in retail, so I can fold clothing and pick stuff up off the floor like a boss.
3. I'm lighthearted and like to laugh.
4. I'm not afraid of a challenge. (Now this isn't actually true, but I fake it well, and can appear quite brave when really

I'm fighting back the nervous diarrhea.)

5. I make a mean box of macaroni and cheese.
6. I've never been arrested.

"Tell me why you'd be well-suited for the job of being a mom?" I imagine them asking.

"Well," I brag. "I've never been arrested."

Upon quick inspection, my list seems woefully lacking, and honestly, having been arrested probably has no bearing on whether or not someone will make a good mother. And it's not like I'd never had the opportunity to be arrested, I just hadn't been caught. I pragmatically decide to keep this to myself.

What am I doing here? I begin to panic. *I can't walk out,* I think, doing that pretending to be brave thing I mentioned earlier. So I smile and try to ignore the bead of perspiration that snakes its way down my spine, blessedly stopping just before my crack.

"Tell me about the last time you changed a diaper." The first question is lobbed to me after introductions and weather-related chit chat. They think they're starting off easy.

"Uh, well, I watched my husband change our niece's diaper three years ago," I offer. "I handed him a wipe, I think." Seeing their faces, I hurriedly add, "I babysat in high school! I changed diapers back in the nineties!"

The women all make a quick note on their notepads.

"Okay, how are you at managing your work and home responsibilities on very little sleep?"

I laugh. They do not.

"Oh, sorry, I thought you were joking." I'm not ready to lie this early in the interview. "I don't work on very little sleep. Sleep is important. Haven't you guys heard that sleep is, like, crucial to a healthy lifestyle?" I did not mention that what with all of my happy hours and poor eating habits, I really needed this sleep thing to keep me balanced. Because I care about my body, that's why.

Their pens scratch furiously.

"How patient are you?" The question is asked in a way that suggests they already know they won't be impressed by my answer.

I Still Just Want to Pee Alone

"I'd say I'm an eight."

They brighten. "On a scale of one to ten?"

"Oh, my bad. That's on a scale of one to one hundred. I'm not terribly patient." I continue, "Especially when I'm waiting for someone to get ready. I'm all, 'What the hell? Get your damn shoes on!'" I'm surprised by the question. Is patience an important trait for parents?

"So you swear?" one asks.

"And yell?" another pipes in.

I sigh. "Yeah. Sorry for the language. I do that. And yes to the yelling. Only when I'm pissed, though. Or when I'm talking on the phone. My husband says I talk super loud on the phone." I grinned, giving them the "Husbands, am I right?" shrug.

Looking for a safe question, they peruse the list. Encouragingly, one offers, "How do you feel about chicken nuggets?"

"I love them!" I smile enthusiastically. "My husband and I always hit the Wendy's drive-through on our way home from the bar. It's hard to beat a nugget straight out of the fryer."

"How about cold nuggets that are half eaten with the breading sucked off? And while we're at it, are you willing to eat cold fries dipped in ketchup? Don't worry, the ketchup is licked off. You need to eat the fries and nuggets or else they end up on the floor and your dog will eat so many he'll puke. Speaking of puke, where do you stand on catching vomit with your bare hands?"

I stare, feeling the armpit faucets turning on. "Good?" I choose this question rather than lying my face off, completely unconvincingly.

Attempting to bring it back, they toss me what they think will be a softball. "You like to snuggle, right?"

"Weeelllll," I falter, "Sort of. I mean, my mom said I wasn't very snuggly as a baby, and I like to cuddle with my husband, but not for long because I get hot, and my arm cramps up, and my legs feel trapped, and … " I look at the faces of the women across the table and blurt, "I can't help it! I'm claustrophobic!"

Finally, the woman in the center leans in. "I have to know," she asks, gently. "Why are you here? You don't like to snuggle. You don't change diapers. You yell, you're impatient, and you swear —even in an interview. You can't function without a full night's sleep. Did you even read the job description?"

I let her question sink in.

"I did. And I'm not sure I want to do this job. My friends tell me I'll like it. They say I'll love it, even when I hate it, and that intrigues me. I like holding little hands, and I like reading Shel Sliverstein. I make a killer mac and cheese, and my husband can change the hell out of a diaper. I like adventure and I also like staying in on a Saturday night. I like elastic waistbands, and I hear that your boobs get really big when you're pregnant. My A-cups like the sound of that. I am a fast learner and even though the pay blows, I'll bet I can do my current job and this mom thing, too."

The three women look at each other and smile.

"Amy Flory?"

Hearing my name, I'm pulled back to reality; to the OB/GYN waiting room and to the uncomfortable chair I'm sitting in, and my eyes settle on a woman a few chairs away, her hands resting on her enormous belly. She sees me touch my still-flat stomach, the one that won't be flat for long, and she offers a nod and a smile.

I smile back as I stand and walk in to the appointment where I'll hear my baby's heartbeat for the first time.

I can do this.

AMY FLORY is a contributor to the popular books The Big Book of Parenting Tweets, "You Have Lipstick on Your Teeth," I Just Want to Pee Alone, *and* I Just Want to Be Alone. *She has been featured on multiple parenting sites, and was named one of Mashable's 17 Funny Moms on Twitter in 2013, and World's Meanest Mom by her kids in 2014. You can find Amy sharing slow cooker recipes and embarrassing stories about herself and her family at* FunnyIsFamily.com.

Flames, Knives and Fear: A Family Dinner
By Kim Forde
The Fordeville Diaries

There are phrases you say as a parent that come from a place of complete desperation or delusion. And the moment you speak the words out loud, you know you are making a mistake of epic, regrettable proportions.

Things like, "Sure, you can take out the Play-Doh while I'm in the other room."

Or, "I saw some great birthday cake ideas on Pinterest."

And then there was a recent favorite of mine: "Hey, let's all go out to dinner!"

I said it almost with a sing-songy, cheerleader-ish quality that was, in retrospect, more to convince myself than any other family members that my plight was worthwhile. I wasn't looking for a fancy night out by any stretch. It was a regular Saturday to wrap up a regular week and, frankly, I just needed a change of scenery. I needed to be the one not preparing the food, not cleaning up the table, and definitely not negotiating the border control between food groups touching each other on my kids' plates.

I wanted, for one night, to be on the receiving end of service and the production end of the part where you sit down and chew food.

I wanted out of my kitchen.

Now, to be clear, I had seen this movie before. I knew that taking my kids (ages seven, five, and one) out to eat is not for the faint of heart. It requires skill, finesse, patience and, above all, the ability to cut food with one hand while drinking wine with the other. (Husband = designated driver.)

On this particular night, after my suggestion to go to a restaurant, my husband looked squarely at me with a raised eyebrow that silently said, "You have completely lost your shit, but I will play along since you're clearly not going to cook anything here tonight."

(Subtitle: "Do not complain to me later when you cannot look any town resident in the eye who dined in the same room with our children.")

If you have small children, you know how it is—that terrifyingly fine line between confidence, ambivalence, and anxiety over how this meal in public is going to go down. The real problem is that, once in about every thirty-two attempts, the whole ordeal goes kind of O.K. and nobody wants to kill each other and you get lulled into a false sense of security that maybe you've hit that point where it just might be getting easier.

NO. NOT TRUE. Listen to me very carefully: these are evil lies that our brains tell us when we have no groceries or wine left at home.

Because, really, is anything with a one-year-old in tow going to be remotely approaching the "getting easier" phase? Sure. Relative to a scene from *Braveheart*, maybe.

And yet, every now and then, I make the attempt.

This time, I thought maybe we could try something new and mix it up for the kids. Why drag them to a buffet where I must play Whack-a-Mole with their little hands grubbing after the common food source? And clearly we weren't aiming for fine dining. Sure, I could have gone to a kid-themed restaurant but, damn it, it's my night too. What could possibly keep them entertained while my husband and I eat an adult-ish meal?

A hibachi grill.

I remembered I had an unused Groupon for a hibachi place near our house. Then I learned that it was Kids Eat Free Night. These must be signs.

I figured my kids would marvel at the fun hibachi displays that the chefs put on. You know, a little knife throwing. Some fire. Tossing food into patrons' mouths. Hell, it's not unlike how we eat at home.

Plus, there was a big bar at this place. Just saying.

And so, I began my preparations. Because you just don't walk into a battle unarmed.

Now—and this is important—the trick is not to *appear* insane in one's prep. I packed the diaper bag—you know, the one that looks casual, average-size and carefree from the outside, like a normal person would tote. But helllll, no—its hidden contents secretly rival that of an FAA-mandated checked bag for a trip that twice circles the Earth.

I Still Just Want to Pee Alone

People, I have everything except a tent in there, but I'd never let you know from your dining perch. I need you to believe, at least until my party has betrayed me completely somewhere around the entree, that we don't need a bag of tricks to enjoy a simple family meal.

Because who really wants to wear their crazy on their sleeve?

Inside my Secret Bag of Crazy, I had an arsenal of baby distractions, with the items grouped into tiers:

1. Everyday toys (everything is fine).
2. Go-to favorites (borderline crisis).
3. Secret stash (CODE RED—GET THE CHECK, GET THE DAMN CHECK, STAT).

The two older kids still needed a few things in the bag to stay out of trouble, like some books, along with Stormtroopers who were fully prepared to battle Disney Princesses to the death on a bread plate. I distributed these items with a long, *I-mean-it* stare and reviewed, in pointed detail, the rules we laid out on the drive over. This may or may not have included a bribe for extra screen time later at home. (Of course it did.)

I strapped the baby into the shaky, questionable high chair that was probably covered in plague spores, and then began the cardio component of my meal: entertaining him. (Upside: burning calories as I consume them.)

I looked around the restaurant and, inevitably, recognized a handful of local families. This meant a quick mental assessment of how much I cared about alienating them forever before they reached dessert. Like any student of rationality, I arrived at the following formula, based strictly on random female mood volatility driven by sleep deprivation:

1. If my care level is in the medium-to-high range, a quick dose of friendly small talk is in order to minimize the collateral damage.
2. If you tried to sucker me into a crappy role with the school fundraiser last week, I remain seated and wait for the shit show to play out within your hearing range.

Once I completed this highly scientific evaluation and determined we'd have at least one less holiday party to attend next December, my husband and I began the ordering process. You know the process, people with small children, the one where all of the food for the entire excursion gets ordered upfront. Where your first drink has traveled with you from the waiting area to the table, in the name of efficiency. Where appetizers become optional at best so that we have more than a snowball's chance in hell of chewing our entrees. Where kids' desserts are strictly stalling tactics to buy silence and time for us to finish our cocktails in peace. Where we are basically asking for the check before you've poured us any water. Where, if you'd let us, we would have ordered every morsel of our food and its ridiculous kid-specifications two weeks ago on the Internet. Food for thought: If you would just upgrade your technology, you would barely have to interact with us at all.

As we placed our order and got situated at our hibachi table, I have to say that I was feeling pretty pleased with myself for coming up with this idea. New experience for the kids. Booze for the parents. Fried rice for all!

What could be bad about this?

Please, stand back and let me count the ways.

First: Never, ever go somewhere during Kids Eat Free Night. Ever. I honestly can't believe I made such a rookie mistake. The noise level was just beyond anything the human ear can tolerate. If you don't believe me, let me explain it another way: My kids had their hands glued to their ears. *My kids. Thought it was too noisy.* Oh, the irony. And the schadenfreude. You can't hear yourselves think, kids? Heyyyyyy, what's that like?

Also? It turns out that the knife tossing and fire display were not entertainment as much as, shall we say, abject terror for my older kids. I don't have a real photo to share from the evening, but I can paint a detailed mental picture that will give you a fair indication. You know those horror movie posters with kids covering their eyes and long, distorted stretched faces? That. I could have posted it on Instagram, using the Fright Night filter.

I Still Just Want to Pee Alone

Between flame throwing, I noticed that Round 1 of the Older Sibling Standoff had gotten underway. Right on schedule! I reminded myself this is just the warm-up. It's not time to have the evening ruined for at least another thirty-eight minutes.

Speaking of pacing, I was slightly surprised to see that the baby was on Level Two of the diaper bag contents already. Things were getting shifty and escalating. It was at this point when I saw my husband mistakenly reach for a Level Three toy. Our eyes met as he realized, with a sweaty brow, what such an error could have cost us this early in the meal.

So, there were my older kids. Ears covered, whining, and slightly cowering. The chef, having zero experience with either kids or humanity in general, did not smile or even generally acknowledge that they think he's going to filet them. His next move could have gone one of several ways. Like toning it down a touch. Or directing his glance at the table's other patrons, who didn't appear to have their lives flashing before their young eyes.

Not our chef. He went all Eye of the Tiger and decided to instead pull out the big guns.

And so began the inevitable hibachi game of "catch this piece of food in your mouth." Cute for those who understand. A crowd favorite, even. But my kids, unfortunately, thought they were being assaulted with steaming hot shrimp and chicken by a pyromaniac disguised in a chef's uniform. More screaming ensued.

"No fire!"

"Don't throw that food at me!"

"It's soooo loud in heeeeere!"

"Fire! Fire! Noooo!"

I mentioned they had a big bar, right?

The baby, although on his forty-seventh Houdini attempt to escape from the high chair, was the only one of my children not traumatized by this entire situation. I believe that it is his proven quest-for-danger-at-all-costs mentality that led him to seek out direct eye contact with the The Chef of Fire. Sort of an unspoken mano a mano acknowledgment and nod of respect. Or perhaps an aspirational glance that said, "I, too, can grow up to throw knives and flames and food, despite my current domestic restrictions."

The flames began to die down as we ate our meal, and for a few minutes, we had reverted back from Crisis Mode to standard crappy behavior. It was at this point that perhaps my biggest disappointment of the evening occurred: My children didn't like the fried rice. My frustration was palpable and it brought up a lot of questions deep in my soul. Are genetics a hoax? And what kind of people am I raising here? I just didn't have the answers.

And just when my husband and I felt we had managed them through all of the evening's trauma, the final chapter began: the birthday songs.

Ohhhh, shit. Waitress! Refill, please!

Have you seen the hibachi approach to birthdays? It's usually over the top. In this particular version of my kids' personal hell, it involved a strobing disco light, loud music (more noise, yay!), and an employee with a big light-up hat who grabbed the guest of honor by his raised arms, and repeatedly yelled "Banzai!" The birthday boy in the restaurant seemed to enjoy this. Most of the patrons smiled, clapped and even yelled in unison.

Except for my pint-sized party of fried rice haters. This was the last straw for them. They were horrified. They thought this boy was being attacked.

"Why is that man grabbing the boy by the arms? He's screaming at him! What's happening?"

"It's so loud!"

"Is there going to be more fire? Please, no more fire!"

Last call for Mom and Dad, please. And a referral to the nearest children's therapist.

When the trauma was over, we left the place with the kids still covering their ears and asking a lot of questions about everyone's well being and the importance of fire safety. Once in the safe haven of our car, my son made an impassioned plea to us: if he behaved all of the time, would we promise to never, ever bring him here for his birthday?

I Still Just Want to Pee Alone

So much for something new. All we got was Hibachi PTSD. And a tiny, aspiring flame-thrower.

And so, our plans for the next five hundred Saturday nights are settled: chicken nuggets at home. Right at the corner of Eating With Kids Sucks and Never Leaving the House Again.

KIM FORDE writes about the art of domestic failure on her blog, <u>The Fordeville Diaries</u>. A former Manhattan resident, she is now a secret suburban convert at home with three young kids. Kim has appeared in the NYC production of Listen to Your Mother, and has written for The Huffington Post and Scary Mommy. She was twice named a Humor Voice of the Year by BlogHer and contributed to several humor anthologies, including I Just Want to Be Alone, "You Have Lipstick on Your Teeth," *and* I Just Want to Pee Alone. *When not busy managing her Starbucks addiction and healthy fear of craft stores, she spends more time on <u>social media</u> than she is prepared to admit.*

Here's Mommy!
By Sarah del Rio
est. 1975

Before our son was born, my husband and I fancied ourselves quite the sexy, metropolitan couple.

We lived in our state's largest city, just a few easy minutes from downtown. Our neighborhood was nice, but not *too* nice. It was safe, but not *too* safe. It had upscale boutiques, gallery hops, and artisan bakeries; it also had hookers, drug dealers, and an admirable contingent of twitchy weirdos.

We were never bored in our little urban neighborhood. There was just enough crime to give us a thrill, there was just enough culture to keep us entertained, and there was more than enough opportunity for us to develop the special kind of snobbishness that only city-dwellers can truly manage.

"Psssht, the *suburbs*," we'd scoff, smoking our cigarettes and savoring our craft beers.

"We would *never* move there," we'd declare, strolling hand-in-hand past a masturbating hobo.

"Can you *imagine*?" we'd ask ourselves, walking through the city's central park, listening to the snap, crackle, and pop of used hypodermic needles crunching underfoot. "What an utter *nightmare*."

Then I got pregnant.

Suddenly, my response to the guy selling dime-bags in front of our apartment building went from an overindulgent "Welp, that's just how it is in the city," to a panicked "OH MY GOD, MY SWEET FETUS IS IN TERRIBLE DANGER!" I started to jump at the shadow of every thug, tweaker, and corner hustler. Muggings and car break-ins became major sources of anxiety. Visions of pedophiles danced in my head.

So we moved. For the next couple of years, my husband and I sought solace in a two-story walk-up that was *slightly* farther away from the city, but still close enough to save face with our cool, single, childless friends. But it just wasn't sustainable. Our family was growing. We needed more space. We needed more storage. We needed more security.

I Still Just Want to Pee Alone

Which is why, right before our son turned two, we did it. What we swore we'd never, *ever* do.

We bought a house in the suburbs.

Well, come on! Where else were we going to find a house with three bedrooms and three bathrooms for less than a million billion dollars? Where else were we going to land a place with a decent-sized back yard in which our son could safely play? Where else could we look out the window and not see a landscape adorned with used condoms, fast-food wrappers, and crushed cans of Natty Lite?

The answer was nowhere.

Moving to the 'burbs involved a transition of sorts, one that went above and beyond just the physical relocation itself. An emotional transition, if you will. A *lifestyle* transition. After all, my husband and I had forgotten a lot about what it meant to live in a real house. We found ourselves having to readjust to a surprising amount of small luxuries. Things like parking in an attached garage, instead of out on the street. Not having to carry sweaty armfuls of groceries up three flights of stairs. Doing laundry in our own machines like civilized people.

One of the new and interesting things about living in a house was the security system. Instead of a high-maintenance assortment of security chains, cylinder locks, and jimmy-proof deadbolts, we had *technology* to protect us. We'd come home to our safe suburban neighborhood, pull into the garage, open the door to the house, and *boop-beep-boop!* All was well. It was so easy, we slipped right out of the habit of manually locking and unlocking our doors.

We moved into our new house in early fall, but eventually, winter followed. It was a bad one. Frigid temperatures. Mountains of snow. Treacherous sheets of ice. City-wide shortages of rock salt. Snowplows everywhere.

My two-year-old and I didn't leave the house much that winter. We went the comfy and cozy route, choosing to play indoors rather than go out and brave the nasty elements. Our daily routine incorporated lots of toasty socks, warm baths, and long naps, all punctuated by the reassuring (if noisy) furnace going at full throttle. We lived in our pajamas.

On one particularly cold day that winter, I told my son to sit tight in the living room while I ran out to the garage to grab God-knows-what. Maybe a roll of paper towels? A case of Diet Coke, perhaps? One of those new-fangled light bulbs? Whatever it was, it was something so unimportant, so insignificant, and so trivial that I DO NOT REMEMBER ANYTHING ABOUT IT.

What I do, remember, however, is the door to the garage closing behind me, its metal tongue settling into its cradle with an audible "click."

There isn't much of a lock on that door. Just an insubstantial little knob lock—you know, the kind that every homeowner with a security system completely forgets about? In just a few short months, my husband and I certainly had. Which is why my response to hearing the door shut behind me was to have no response at all. It didn't even occur to me that the knob lock might be engaged, because we never used it.

I calmly finished up whatever business I was taking care of in the garage, but when I went to let myself back in the house—well, I'm sure you've already guessed that I was completely and unequivocally *locked out*. Barefoot, in my pajamas, with no house keys, cell phone, or access to my now-unsupervised toddler.

Shit.

Still—I didn't panic. Not at first. Instead, I scrambled through my mind for options. Some of them were halfway plausible; some of them were downright impossible. I prioritized the plausible ones using a highly-customized algorithm involving such variables as "time to implementation," "amount of drama involved," and "likelihood of actually working." Thanks to Fear® and Adrenaline™, all of this information only took me a few seconds to process, and soon I had come up with four possible plans of attack.

The first one involved calling my son over to the door and seeing if he could unlock it from the inside. Not a bad idea on its face, but remember that my son was only two. He did manage to get to the door, and he did rattle the knob obediently, but the locking mechanism aspect of the situation escaped him completely. (Which was ironic, since it was probably he who locked the door in the first place.) It soon became crystal clear that this approach was not going to succeed.

My second option was to open the garage itself and try to get into the house another way. But after a quick mental inventory, I realized that all of the outside doors were also locked, and since the security system was online, any attempt to break into my own home would only set off the alarms and scare the living shit out of my little son. So that idea was dead in the water.

As was, I soon determined, my third option—opening the garage and running across the street to a neighbor's house to borrow a phone or get help. I absolutely couldn't leave my two-year-old son alone in the house, but even if I could have, it was the middle of the day and my neighbors were all at work. Furthermore, it was the dead of winter, and I was unshod, braless, and wearing pajamas so busted and ratty that they provided warmth to no man.

Which brought me to my fourth and final alternative. The most long-shot, Hail Mary, and "IT'S CRAZY, BUT IT JUST MIGHT WORK!" of all my possible options. It wasn't something I *wanted* to do, believe me—it was the farthest thing from what I *wanted* to do. But I could hear my son becoming more and more unsettled, and truth be told, I had nothing left to try.

I started looking around for an ax.

Panic set in as I discovered that we did not, in fact, have an ax. Why would we? Our property was not in a wooded area. We had nothing to chop. There had never been need of an ax, or even a small hatchet. Nonetheless, I offered up a selection of profanities to my husband for not "being prepared," and made a mental note to bitch at him about it later.

Desperate now, I scanned the rest of the garage. Automotive parts? Not helpful. Seventeen bicycles in various states of disrepair? Useless. I even glanced over my gardening supplies, hoping to see something of use there, but my search came up fruitless. There was no way I was going to get through the door with a trowel. Or a rusted hedge clipper. Or an ancient stack of Burpee Seeds.

Finally, my eyes lit upon something laying on my husband's workbench—an assortment of claw hammers. Ding ding! That might do the trick! I grabbed what looked to be the sturdiest one and approached the door with a medley of fear, hesitance, and dare I say—excitement? After all, I'd never destroyed part of a house before. There was something a little thrilling about the notion.

I knew I couldn't smash the entire door down with just a hammer, or even bust a hole in it big enough to climb through. My only real hope was to create a gap wide enough to stick my hand through, reach the knob lock, and set myself free.

I pressed my face against the door and called to my son. "Honey," I said, "Honey, it's very important that you move as far away as you can right now. Do you understand me?"

"Yes, Mommy," replied a tiny, anxious voice. I waited a moment, listened very intensely, and heard my son go absolutely nowhere.

I tried again. "Sweetheart, I'm serious. Go sit in front of the television or on the couch. Mommy will be inside in just a moment."

"Okay," peeped my son, who continued to stay right where he was. Even at two, he was no dummy. He knew something was up, something sensational and possibly even dangerous, and he didn't want to miss it. After some more cajoling, I finally convinced him to move back about six feet. That was as far away as he was going to go, and I just had to accept it.

I took a deep breath. I raised my hammer. Then, squelching the urge to yell, *"Here's Mommy!"* in a totally psychotic voice, I brought the face of the hammer down on the door as hard as I possibly could.

Exhilarating!

Once I got to it, the process of busting a small hole in the door didn't take very long. The door was made of very cheap, hollow-core material and it splintered easily under my mighty hammer. Working quickly, I gouged out a six-inch opening right next to the doorknob, and with a huge sigh of relief, I slid my hand inside and unlocked the door. Then I ran in and scooped up my baby son, who was obviously very confused about what had just happened, but nonetheless extremely happy to see me.

We had to replace the door, of course. I forced my husband to take care of that. It was only what he deserved, after all, for not stocking the garage with a full complement of axes. Or, you know, a house key.

SARAH DEL RIO is a comedy writer whose award-winning humor blog est. 1975 brings snark, levity, and perspective to the ladies of Generation X. She earns her daily bread as a freelance writer and editor.

Sarah is a regular contributor to BLUNTMoms, and has also been featured on Scary Mommy, In the Powder Room, and the Erma Bombeck Writers' Workshop. She has made multiple appearances on The Huffington Post Parents Best Tweets of the Week List.

Sarah's blog can be found at established1975.com. Like her on Facebook and follow her on Twitter.

I Just Want to Go to the Gynecologist Alone
By Stacey Gill
One Funny Motha

I hadn't seen an OB/GYN since we moved. And, if I was being completely honest, the last time I saw one was most likely the day—lying prone on the hospital table—I gave birth. Everything got a little hazy after that so I couldn't quite remember. It wasn't that I was avoiding it. The problem was I didn't know where to go or where to find the time if I did. After Kate was born we followed the customary migration pattern, moving out of our one-bedroom apartment in New York City to a nice house in the suburbs. Kate was seven months old when we moved, and she was nearly three by the time I first contemplated the possibility of a check up.

The baby, of course, never missed any of her doctors' visits. I'd made an appointment with a new pediatrician the week we moved into the new house. In fact, I got a bunch of referrals from our Realtor before we'd even bought the house. But as with everything after a baby, your needs become secondary.

They may have remained that way for the next eighteen years, but I happened to be on the phone with my longtime friend who didn't have any children, but did have regularly scheduled gynecological appointments, when she mentioned her last visit to me. Leaning against the kitchen countertop trying to shake Kate, who wrapped herself securely around my body at all times, from my leg, I casually stated, "Oh, I haven't been to a gynecologist in *years*."

My friend gasped. "You have to go. You can't put that appointment off anymore. You've got to get checked out. Just in case." The concern in her voice made me a little nervous.

I should make sure I'm not dying at least, I thought. I mean I was pretty sure I wasn't. I didn't *feel* like I was dying of cervical cancer or anything, and I was pretty good at intuiting that sort of thing. Still, three years was a while, and although I didn't have much use for the apparatus anymore, I knew I should take the ole uterus in for a tune-up.

So I pulled out the phone book, opened up to the gynecology section and skimmed for the nearest office. That's the way people did it in the old days, ten years ago. Lucky for me there was one around the corner within walking distance. And, that was how I chose the person with whom I would have the most intimate relationship in my life aside from my husband.

Three weeks later I bounded down the front steps, strapped Kate into her stroller, and set out for my appointment. It was an unusually warm fall day, and as I walked the few blocks to the office the parched, brown leaves crunched under the wheels of the stroller. Turning the corner onto the busy main street, Kate started to squirm and writhe. "Out! Walk."

"We're almost there, see?" I bargained. "There's the building at the top of the hill. When we get there you can walk, okay?" Kate was not a patient child so I picked up the pace, but it was tough to lug both myself and a fifty pound butterball up an incline. By the time we made it to the receptionist's desk, I was sweaty and panting. I tore off my jacket and signed in. The receptionist handed me a stack of new patient forms. *Shit, I forgot about that.* I sat down in one of the standard issue office chairs, hunched over the forms and tore through them, attempting to speed up the process and minimize downtime as Kate dumped magazine after magazine onto the floor. "No, no," I admonished. "Let's pick them up." Leaning over my clipboard, I gathered the magazines while Kate shrieked and ran around a row of chairs.

"C'mere," I pleaded with Kate as I tossed a stack of *American Baby* magazines on the faux wood table in front of me. "Sit next to Mommy so I can finish." She slowly wandered over, but as soon as I reached out to grab her she reeled back and laughed. *Great. It's a game now.*

"Katy girl," I called, patting the chair beside mine. But instead of sitting in the chair, she kneeled and leaned on me as I raced through the forms trying to remember my husband's social security number, his work address, and all medical ailments and diseases suffered by both my maternal and paternal mothers.

"Yook, yook," Kate kept repeating, but I ignored her as I hurried to finish up. Then she raised both hands and, shouting "Mine!," dove for my pen.

With a quick maneuver of my elbow, I blocked her, and without stopping the flow of the ink continued scribbling on the reams of paper. Kate jutted out her bottom lip and started to pout.

"Let Mommy finish. Then we get to see the doctor. One more minute." Kate was about to climb down and wreak more havoc on the waiting room when she spied the little plastic bag filled with Teddy Grahams sticking out of the baby bag. I had packed a bunch of snacks for the occasion and was prepared to ply her with Goldfish, Teddy Grahams, pretzels, anything. Hell, I would've even given her kiddie crack—Capri Sun—to make it through this appointment. But I was uncomfortable with starting out so early in the game. It was a high risk.

For a moment Kate and I locked eyes over the baby bag, our faces no more than a foot apart, as we each calculated our next move. Then Kate broke contact and went for the Grahams. My reflexes were quicker and my need greater, and I managed to pull out a package of Goldfish first. Holding it aloft, triumphantly, I grinned. "Want some Goldfish?"

We couldn't start with Teddy Grahams. Those glazed, little potbellied bears were precious. They had to be parceled out with care. They were the grand prize, the Golden Egg, the *pièce de résistance*, and they had to make it to the examination room as I hadn't packed any kiddie crack. Kate looked at the bag of Goldfish and sneered. In full view of the Teddy Grahams, they were a vile, contemptible, completely sub-standard snack.

I exhaled heavily and held out the bag of Teddy Grahams. *Fine. Have it your way.* Kate clapped with glee and munched away as crumbs collected in the corners of her mouth. I turned in the paperwork and just as I sat back down, she flung the bag at me. She was on the move again. That had bought me one solid minute.

"Stacey?" A nurse called.

"Yes, that's me." I grabbed my jacket, the baby bag, and Kate's hand and hurried down the hall after her. She pointed to a chair in one of the examination rooms where I could leave my belongings and directed me to the bathroom where I could leave my urine sample. *But where could I leave Kate?*

I had no choice but to take her into the bathroom with me as I collected my urine sample. *Great.* "Don't. Touch. *Anything*," I warned, but those words are useless on a toddler, and Kate was already running her hands along the metal handicapped rail, the wall, the door, collecting as many bacteria samples as she could.

"Kate, no, don't touch," I begged. Then she ran over to the sink and began smearing the drips left from the previous occupant all over the counter. *Why do you have to touch things? Why? Why can't you just be still and silent in the corner like a good kid?*

I was running out of tricks fast, but this situation called for immediate intervention. "Here, want a lollipop?" I dug frantically through my purse for the Dum Dum floating on the bottom, unwrapped it, and handed it over. Then I hastily tugged my pants down, squatted over the toilet and shoved the plastic cup between my legs. Quickly but cautiously I peed, watching as the warm yellow liquid filled the cup so I wouldn't piss all over my hand, and that's when I heard it. The crunch. My head immediately shot up.

No, no, no, you don't crunch it! You lick it. How is the lollipop going to last if you bite it? Don't you know how lollipops work?

Before I could pull up my pants Kate had finished the candy and was hanging on the doorknob trying to get out. "Kate, wait. I'm not dressed, and you have to wash your hands."

"No!" she screamed.

"Kate, please. We can't leave until you wash your hands."

"Out!" Kate began violently pulling on the door, rattling it in its frame. I rifled through my purse for the hand sanitizer and squirted some gel into her hands and mine. I took a deep breath and stepped out of the bathroom. *This place could really use a babysitting service.*

In the exam room I undressed, put on a paper robe, and climbed up on the crinkly, butcher-block paper positioned over the padded table. Then we waited. Nearly naked, with my feet dangling off the table in drooping, worn, white socks, I looked around the room. There was absolutely nothing with which to occupy a child. It was just a small, stark, white-walled room with cold tiles and harsh florescent lighting.

Kate circled around and when she found nothing of interest, tottered over, looked up at me and raised her arms over her head. "Up." The table was too high for me to reach down and pick her up, and there really wasn't enough room on it for the two of us. *Couldn't they have some toys in here? It's an OB/GYN's office for Pete's sake. Reproduction is pretty much the whole reason they're in business.*

In their defense, I guess I should mention I've never once seen anyone bring a small child into a gynecological exam before. I suppose they only dealt with kids in theory.

"Want some more Teddy Grahams?" My offer was feeble, but it was all I had. The Teddy Grahams, though, no longer held the same alluring cachet they once did back in the waiting room. They were beneath her now. She had tasted the full, sugary, glory of the lollipop. The ante had been upped.

But I was out. All of my reserves had been exhausted. "How about a book?" It was a pathetic attempt, I know, but I'd only brought one lollipop, and, honestly, I thought that would've been plenty.

Why hadn't I brought a whole goddamn bag of Pixy Stix? Or a case of Capri Suns? Whyyy?

Kate scoffed at my ridiculous suggestion then she reached up and, straining, tried to grab the sterilized medical instruments laid out on the counter. *Oh, Jesus Christ.* "No, don't touch. Those are for the doctor." Luckily she was too short, and instead she turned around, slid down to the floor and started crawling across the room to the far wall. "Kate, get off the floor," I snapped, cringing. "*Please.* It's dirty." She let out a squeal and started scooting even faster. I slouched on the table. *Oh, what the hell. She was practically licking the doorknob in the bathroom. How much worse can this be?* Once she reached the wall, she stood up and stretched her arms to the window. She managed to hook the tips of her fingers onto the windowsill. Still, even teetering on her tippy toes, she was barely able to see out. With her chin tilted all the way up she could only make out the indistinct shapes of the blue-grey clouds in the fading afternoon light. Just as she started to whine, the doctor came rushing in. *Oh, thank God. Let this internment be over.*

After introductions and the perfunctory questions, I laid back on the table, and the doctor started in with her poking and prodding. As she palpated my left breast, Kate's whines grew louder, more insistent. "We're almost done, okay?" I hoped the doctor picked up on the cues and the panic in my voice and started palpating a little quicker because I had to get the hell out of this room before Kate blew. But if the doctor had noticed my child was on the verge of a full-blown meltdown, she showed no signs of it. Kate scrambled over to my side of the table and looked up at me as the doctor made her way around my right breast. "Mooommeeeee, wanna go."

"Yes," I said, looking down at her as I lay trapped on the table. "Soon."

The doctor now stood at the foot of the table and yanked out the stirrups. It was time for the internal. As Kate stared at me, the doctor guided my feet into the hard, metal contraptions and had me scoot down to the very end of the table. Then she took up her position between my legs, nose to perineum, and just as she was about to insert the speculum Kate demanded to be picked up. *Um, can't really do that right now. I'm kinda in the middle of a pelvic exam.*

It was clear Kate was very near the edge. So I did the one thing I could from that position flat on my back with a cold metal implement jammed up my hooha. I began to sing.

"I love you. You love me. We're a happy family … "

My voice quavered a little, but I pressed on.

Not once at any point during this entire horrifying episode did anyone on the office staff try to intervene on my behalf. They didn't try to distract Kate so I could focus on the nauseating discomfort of the pelvic exam alone. They didn't offer treats or stickers or candy. They abandoned me in my paper robe, spread eagle on the table, holding Kate's hand as I looked into her innocent eyes and sang the Barney theme song while someone was elbow deep up my insides.

Over and over and over I sang those awful, schmaltzy lyrics. I sang them through the entire pelvic exam, my enthusiasm and inflection eventually giving way to a more rote, mechanical expression. I sang them after the doctor had left the room. I sang them as I rose slowly from the exam table and stared blankly into space. I even sang them as I stoically gathered my clothes and hugged them to my body. Looking back, I believe, I was suffering from PTSD. And, I think, that day a little piece of my soul died.

I've always harbored a singular hatred for that dopey, purple dinosaur. How did he get his own show with his ridiculous, goofy chuckle and useless, atrophied arms? He couldn't even *do* anything. No waving, clapping, hugging, pointing, high fiving or even moving for that matter. He was an overweight, unrealistic hack with non-functioning limbs. And his songs sucked.

From that day forward I vowed no more Barney. No more gynecological appointments with audiences. In fact, no more kids. If this was what I had to go through, I didn't want any more. I should've had them remove my uterus right there on the table. I should have refused to leave the office until every last bit of my reproductive organs were wrenched from my body because I was *never* going through that again.

I was also never going back to that practice. I couldn't. I needed to block this whole horrible episode from my mind if I was ever going to heal. Or see a gynecologist again.

STACEY GILL is an award-winning journalist and the mastermind behind the humor blog, One Funny Motha. Her work has appeared on The Huffington Post, BlogHer, Mom365, The Good Men Project, Scary Mommy and Mommyish among others. In 2014 she was named one of the Top 10 Funny Parent Bloggers of the Year by VoiceBoks. Perhaps most importantly, she is the proud founder of the Detached Parenting Movement, a child-rearing model she single-handedly developed without any guidance or advanced degrees in child psychology. Currently, she's at work on a memoir fully exploring this parenting style.

It's Not Pee. It's You.
By Michelle Back
Mommy Back Talk

There's a lot of vagina talk when you're pregnant. Do you have crotch ache? Can't get enough of/can't stand your husband? And just how are you planning on getting that baby out of there? We all know how the baby got there and now we want to know how it's going to come out. For most babies, they come out the way they went in—through a vagina. This is what I wanted. When anyone inquired about how I would deliver, I told them: natural birth. The conversation usually went something like this:

Lady (men never ask about birth): So how do you think you'll deliver?

Me: I'm planning on a natural birth.

Lady: Just ask for your epidural early. No sense in suffering.

Me: I'm thinking of giving it a go the old-fashioned way.

Lady: Wow, you're brave. *(You're fucking nuts.)*

Me: We'll see. If it gets too bad, I guess I'll get some drugs. *(I'm not taking drugs. Challenge accepted.)*

I told everyone who asked the same thing: no drugs. My husband was on the bandwagon, too, and he would tell people the plan whenever the chance arose for him (I guess men *do* talk about birth). We've been through a major house renovation together, and he has seen and been surprised by my strength and determination under duress. I demolished our kitchen and pulled out a poured marble countertop in our master bath (and then promptly realized that it was really fucking heavy, but I was already holding it, so I shimmied it down to the ground with a lot of grunting—practically just like giving birth). I've also sliced open my index finger with a utility knife while trying to cut a sheet of drywall. If these things don't qualify me for natural birth, I don't know what does. I knew I had stamina and I knew I could handle pain. I figured if I could handle pain one million times worse than anything I've experienced, I'd be good to go. Also, at some point in my pregnancy, I watched *The Business of Being Born* and that sealed the deal. Drugs were the devil. Bring it on.

At the very beginning of my pregnancy, though, I should have realized that I was not in charge. I was ten days late when I finally found out I was pregnant. It's not that I hadn't been paying attention to my cycles that had been regular since the first day Aunt Flo had darkened my lady bits' door step over twenty years ago. When she was late, I took notice. I wanted to be pregnant, but without a positive test, I thought I had gone through spontaneous menopause. My OB/GYN was dumbfounded. By the time I got that positive pregnancy test, though, I had started to form my birth plan. Now all I had to do was wait.

Well, I guess my vagina got wind of this natural birth plan and formed an alliance with my daughter and uterus. At thirty-two weeks, my daughter started a painful turn inside me. She flipped from the perfect birthing position to breech. With that maneuver, my birth plan was null and void. My vagina was off the hook. Not only would I be needing drugs for my delivery, I would also be having a C-section.

I tried with futility to get my daughter to flip back to the proper position. I placed a bag of frozen peas on the top of my belly every evening. The cold was supposed to make the baby want to flip her head away from the cold, because everyone knows that babies much prefer to have cold feet than to have a cold head. The only thing the cold ever did was make her move to the side a little, while I sat there nearly giving myself frostbite. I also tried elevating my pelvis. This was supposed to make the heaviest part of the baby pop up into your pelvis while you are precariously balancing yourself almost upside down on an ironing board that you've propped up against the couch to give it just the right incline (super-duper safe and there's no way you look the least bit ridiculous doing this). This method didn't work either. The only thing it accomplished was giving me the worst heartburn in the history of the world. Also, spoiler alert: my daughter had a tiny head by newborn standards. If ever there was baby who should have passed through the birth canal, it was her. It would have been practically painless, vagina. Thanks a lot.

We were planning on having more than one kid, though, so I figured I could push out the next one.

I Still Just Want to Pee Alone

At thirty-nine weeks, my husband and I went to my weekly prenatal appointment. It was exactly a week before my daughter was due. We decided to schedule the C-section a few days after my due date because what first baby ever comes early? My OB/GYN also said that my cervix in no way looked like it was about to release the life inside me, so I shouldn't worry about going into labor early. (Poor woman, she should have known better.) We scheduled the C-section for a week and a half away. I figured I would take advantage of the time I had until then. I was going to finish up all my work in the next few days and then take some time for myself. I was going to get a pedicure, pack a hospital bag, and take a lot of naps. My husband and I were going to eat out every night. My husband was going to install the car seat in our brand-new family car. We would be totally prepared for the arrival of our daughter. I'd greet her showered and rested, and my toes would look fabulous.

The weekend following our appointment, I decided to scrub the tile floor in the kitchen. I felt energized and secure in knowing that we had a week until our baby would come. Not only would I have fabulous toes, but my kitchen floor would be pristine for the day we brought our little bundle home. It didn't occur to me until later (possibly a year later) that the burst of energy should have clued me in that the end was nigh. I had somehow overlooked or completely forgotten that a sudden burst of energy can be a sign that labor is imminent.

Very early Monday morning, just four days after my last prenatal appointment, a week before my scheduled C-section, and several days before my due date, I woke up to pee for the fortieth time. I sat down on the toilet and a gush of water came out of me. Given the early hour, it took me a minute to realize that the gush probably wasn't pee. Barely awake, I thought back to our birthing class, remembering that if you can stop the flow of water, it's pee. I did a few Kegels and the flow stopped each time (way to go lady bits!), but something was making me think that possibly, maybe my water had just broke … on the toilet. I got up, flushed, sat down again, got up, and flushed about four times. I washed my hands and waddled back to bed. It crossed my mind that something really gross had come out-of-me the night before, which was probably my mucus plug (gag!), setting this whole thing in motion. We already had plan B in place, though, so I was not letting myself believe that "it was time." I climbed into bed and as I settled into my pillow, my husband asked if everything was O.K. I casually said, "I think my water broke." Having his wits about him, he jumped up and told me that we need-ed to go to the hospital and that I needed to call the doctor. I sat up and tried to figure out what the hell I was supposed to do now. My bag wasn't packed. I still had unfinished tasks at work. We hadn't in-stalled the car seat. Most importantly, there was no way I would have time to get a pedicure, and I probably wasn't going to have a final shower either.

My plans for a relaxing final week of pregnancy had just been doused in amniotic fluid. I called my doctor and told her that I thought my water broke, but I couldn't be certain. I got out of bed, leaking and focusing on the only task I knew I could handle at the moment. (No, not a shower, which would have been the right thing to do.) I asked my husband to grab me a puppy pad we have on hand for our Chihuahua so I could sit down at my desk to e-mail everyone I was working with to let them know that I was possibly, maybe in labor. Nearly two hours later, after my husband had taken a shower, arranged for his dad to pick up our dogs, packed my hospital bag, taken out the trash, and whatever else he was in a frenzy about, he walked into my home office and said, "It's time to go." I swallowed, said something about not being able to get an e-mail to send, and stood up. More water came out of me. This whole time I hadn't ad-mitted that it wasn't pee. It was time to face the music. It wasn't pee; it was my daughter telling me that she was ready to meet us, even if it didn't fit the plan, any of the plans.

We gathered up our bags and walked out to the car. I stopped suddenly on our front walk and yelled, "The car seat! We need the car seat!" Here we were walking out the door with just our luggage like we were leaving on vacation, and we were about to forget the damn car seat—we were clearly prepared to become parents.

I Still Just Want to Pee Alone

On the way to the hospital my OB/GYN called: "Hi, Michelle, are you at the hospital? I haven't seen you check in yet." I laughed a little, "It took us a bit to leave the house (because I'm in deep denial). We'll be there in about ten minutes."

A lot happened in those ten minutes. I called my Dad who I knew would be awake to let him and my mom know that it was time. He didn't believe me at first, like I was pranking him at five forty-five in the morning. Trust me, Dad, I couldn't believe it either. And it really finally hit me full force: this was it. We were going to the hospital to have a baby who surprised us in her own little way by showing up late in the beginning and early in the end.

Once at the hospital, everything happened very quickly. About forty-five minutes after we arrived, our daughter was born. She screamed and had dark hair and chubby cheeks. She was perfect.

One thing I had overlooked in all of this is that C-sections are surgery. Like real surgery. It never occurred to me how painful it might be to recover from a C-section. My vagina might have been no worse for wear, but I still felt tore up from the floor up.

After we were home, my husband told me: "I already knew this, but when I saw you get out of bed for the first time at the hospital, I thought, 'Ladies, you all are some tough-ass bitches.'" Ain't it the truth? We can withstand an incredible amount of pain to bring a little one into our lives who can make us incredibly happy sometimes and at other times make us wonder why we ever thought procreating was a good idea. We can even forgive them for interrupting a pee before they're even here.

MICHELLE BACK is a writer, editor, blogger, and mother who decided to get serious about writing by starting her blog Mommy Back Talk in June 2014. She writes humorously about raising a toddler and finding her footing as a mother. Michelle has a two-year-old daughter and a carefully crafted Netflix queue, and if she spent as much time tending to other things in her life as she does mothering her daughter and crafting her queue, she could rule the world. She also likes red wine, dark chocolate, French fries, her iPhone, Facebook, and Instagram. Her husband is pretty O.K., too.

Reading, the Killer of Innocence
By Courtney Fitzgerald
Our Small Moments

I am a lover words. I remember writing all words I knew, for fun, sitting at our family kitchen table. I loved reading them, stringing words together to make stories and live in other worlds. I also loved creating new words from other ones. The written word has always held a special place in my heart, that is, until my kids started reading. That's when I realized that words are meant to be both admired and feared.

As soon as I was handed the role of motherhood, I took my title seriously. I wanted nothing more than to shelter my kids from the bad stuff out there, and keep them young and pure for as long as possible. It never occurred to me that sharing my love of words with my kids would be the cause of their innocent worlds crumbling down around their feet.

My son read before he talked. For years, before we understood him, he'd point to words in the store and say something we couldn't understand. As soon as he learned to talk, we realized the indecipherable things he said were the words he was pointing to around the stores. We were amazed and proud of our hyperlexic three-year-old reader.

My daughter, also learned to read rather young. As soon as her older brother was in kindergarten, and it was just the two of us all day, I taught her how to read. She was ready, we had the time, and I missed my role as a teacher. It was a wonderful arrangement full of the alphabet song, rhyming words, and finding words to identify everywhere we went. In hindsight, that is where I went wrong, teaching my free-spirited daughter to look for words in our everyday world.

In the beginning of their literate lives, it was a pat on the I-am-such-a-good-parent's back when we walked the streets of Boston and my kids shouted, "Commercial Street! Congress! Fenway!" My husband and I were so proud, smug, and sure of ourselves in those moments.

The real lessons, about the dangers of literate children, were learned not walking down big city streets, but in our small, conservative, Midwestern town. Before I tell you a few, horrifying stories about my literate kids, please remember this lesson: do not, I repeat, do NOT teach your children to find words out in public, especially when you take them to playgrounds, drive them down country roads, or walk through the stores.

One spring afternoon, I took my children to the park. The kids were playing and I was reading, so it was a typical outing. I was happily lost in words, as I heard my kids playing with other kids.

My mind heard my daughter's question to her brother, before I realized what it meant. "Buddy, what does this word say?"

"Mooom, what does f*ck mean?" my son yelled from across the playground.

Ahhh! my mother mind screamed. My stomach immediately flipped. I knew this day was coming, but I did not think it would happen at a playground. "Buddy, come here," was my first instinct. He ran over.

"What does it mean?" he asked innocently.

"Umm ... hmm, well, it's a *naughty* word. Probably the naughtiest word ever made, so don't say it, EVER."

"But what does it mean?"

He was not going to let this drop, and wanted an answer. "You are not ready to know what it means, you just have to believe me that you should never, ever say it, use it, or think it. Please let it go."

He ran back to the other kids, and I hoped the whole thing was over. The next minute I heard, "Buddy, what did Mommy say f*ck means?" my daughter asked loud enough for everyone to hear again.

As I ran over to my kids, I noticed other mothers gathering their kids, trying to leave the park. *Great, now we are* that *family, the one who teaches other kids profanity at the park.* I had the same conversation with my daughter and hoped that we were done with that word. As I talked to my kids, I noticed a few other one syllable words written not far away, so I decided that our fun outing at this park was over, before my kids shouted them.

I forgave myself for their immature reading skills, until a few days later when we were driving across the prairie, which is home to numerous conservative billboards.

"What does ab-or-tion mean?"

Seriously? My husband and I looked at each other. We did not need to speak, we were both wondering the same thing, *How are we going to get around this one?* We both waited a few minutes, hoping the other would handle this serious question.

"Umm, hmm, umm, well ... " I stammered looking for the right words to say. "Well, you know what, Buddy, I do not know what that word means." I pretended to think. "Hmm."

My husband gave me the, *Are you kidding me?* look, and I replied with a *You didn't say anything* glare.

"Can you look it up?" Buddy asked.

I looked at my cheap smartphone. "Oh, bummer, no service. We are not meant to know. Case closed." Luckily, on that day, my son accepted the fact he was not going to know the meaning of that word he saw many times as we drove down the country roads.

The straw that finally broke my back, happened at the grocery store. My daughter and I were picking up a few things, but we had lots of time, so we strolled through the aisles, collecting the things we came for, and a million others that I suddenly remembered we "needed."

I was standing in the feminine hygiene product aisle, comparing prices on the items I needed, when I felt a tug.

I looked down, and there was my four-year-old daughter holding a box and a small squirt bottle.

"Look what I found, Mommy! This one says K-Y, just like the letters in the alphabet!"

My face turned white, as my jaw dropped to my knees.

"And this one," she held up the box, "says, Tr-o-j-an ... c-on-d—"

I grabbed the items out of her hand, and threw them on a nearby shelf.

"Never mind those things! Now, I think we need to be done reading words for awhile. Oh, look cookies! Let's get some!"

I Still Just Want to Pee Alone

From that point on, until my little girl went to kindergarten, I stopped letting her read to me. I still read to her, but I was not going to be responsible for her teaching her whole preschool class about condoms, cussing, KY, and abortions. We had standards after all.

COURTNEY FITZGERALD is a mom to two readers, a widow, a teacher, a writer, and a dreamer. She loves to make people laugh, but people love it when when she makes them cry. Courtney writes honestly about her perfectly imperfect family at Our Small Moments*. Her work has been featured on sites like The Huffington Post, Mamalode, and Autism Speaks. She was a speaker at BlogU '14. She wrote an essay about marriage that is in the hit anthology,* I Just Want to Be Alone*. Follow her on* Facebook, Twitter, Pinterest, *and* Instagram*.*

Shuddup & Fockoff
By Linda Roy
elleroy was here

"I just spent five of the longest hours of my life hosting my kid's playdate. The house looks like the aftermath of Hurricane Katrina, the dog is hiding under the end table, and there's a trail of empty juice boxes leading from my son's room to the front door. I need a shot of Tequila and a lie down. Won't somebody please help me?"

- Tired Housewife, somewhere in New Jersey

Attention, Mothers: Are you or someone you love suffering from PTPS? Post Traumatic Playdate Syndrome (PTPS) is the leading cause of all other syndromes in America. That's why you need the legal team of Shuddup & Fockoff. We specialize in bad playdate litigation. We'll work hard to get you the compensation you deserve.

If you've ever been subjected to the kind of senseless destruction that bad playdates can inflict, you know the damage it can cause, both financially and emotionally. The law offices of Shuddup & Fockoff understand this. For over forty years, we've worked with traumatized playdate hosts to bring other people's kids and their clueless parents to justice.

"I'm Brandon Fockoff. If you've ever had your house ransacked by a group of unruly six year olds, you *know* you'll never get back all those hours you spent unclogging toilets, picking up Legos, and trying to clean Kool Aid out from underneath the refrigerator. The attorneys at Shuddup & Fockoff specialize in domestic playdate disputes of all kinds. There's no case we won't argue; no claim we won't tackle. We'll fight to put an end to PTPS."

Here's one woman's testimonial:

"For years I've put up with other people's kids trashing my house. They go through my cupboards, raid my refrigerator, destroy everything and leave me with a headache the size of a Buick. My Tyler goes to his friends' houses, but we end up having to reciprocate. When I'd finally had enough, I called Shuddup & Fockoff. They got me the settlement I needed. Now I don't have to worry about other people's kids, or their parents crossing my threshold ever again. Sure, Back to School Nights are awkward, but

*it's worth it. I got new wall-to-wall carpeting and a trip to St. Barts! Thank
you, Shuddup & Fockoff."*

At Shuddup & Fockoff, we care about your playdate tragedies.
So if you've ever hosted a sleepover that got out of hand or been del-
uged with requests from other people's kids for food they don't eat, if
your new lamp has gone out the window along with your sanity,
we'll fight tirelessly to substantiate your claim. Because you have
enough to worry about; like how you're going to get Dorito dust off
of your brand new sofa.

We've handled all sorts of claims, so we know how to deal with
the defendant and their dependents.

So if this sounds familiar:

- Parents who drop off multiple children for indeterminable
  amounts of time so they can go to Starbucks
- The scattering of every one of your child's toys to the farthest
  reaches of your home.
- The "poop in the wastebasket" incident.
- The kid who refuses to leave, staging a standoff in your bed-
  room.
- The kid who terrorizes the family dog.
- Kids who invite themselves over for dinner.
- Parents who invite themselves *and* their children over for din-
  ner.
- The biters, hair pullers, and high pitched screamers.
  We can help. We're experts in helping PTPS victims get the
  piece of mind they're entitled to.

We have offices across the country. Call 1-800-BAD-PLD8 now,
to get what's coming to you. Because no one should have to live with
the debilitating after effects of bad playdates.

Sometimes the only recourse is Shuddup & Fockoff.

elleroy was here

LINDA ROY is the wisecracking musician behind the blog <u>elleroy was here</u>. She lives in New Jersey with her husband and two boys who swear she's the female Larry David. A 2014 BlogHer Voice of the Year for Humor, she has contributed to The Huffington Post, Scary Mommy, In the Powder Room, Erma Bombeck Writers' Workshop, Humor Outcasts, BlogHer, Mamapedia, BonBon Break, Midlife Boulevard, and Aiming Low. She is co-author of the humor anthologies Clash of the Couples, Motherhood May Cause Drowsiness, *and the upcoming* Surviving Mental Illness Through Humor. *No wonder her family is always running out of clean underwear.*

Encore!
By Susan Lee Maccarelli
Pecked To Death by Chickens

My four-year-old daughter recently got a flier in her preschool take home folder about an "Encore" program offered at her school called "Junior Lego Structural Engineering for Pre-Kindergarten." I initially put it aside, figuring that this weekly event would unfold somewhere along the lines of "Advanced Coding for Wombats." Once my husband saw the registration form, however, his love of colored bricks and tiny people with snap-on hair got the better of him, and she was enrolled the next day.

As Liana indulged her inner architect with the Lego class, I indulged my inner QVC-watcher as her typical four hour school day stretched to five and a half with the extra class. I've never had a non-family member babysit my kids, but this was paying a teacher for babysitting, under the guise of enrichment—which I believe is genius.

Lego's came to a painful halt after six weeks, and I was left desperately researching other course options for small people on the Internet. I needed to find a win-win situation where I felt good about the subject matter and she enjoyed it, in order to make sure this college for kids idea would continue to work for me in the future.

The first option I came across was Itsy-Bitsy Yoga. As I thought it through, I realized that Liana sleeps in child's pose and watches television in downward dog. I'm pretty sure she's more flexible than any thirty-something teaching the class, plus I don't need her being exposed to yoga pants at such an early age. I wasn't phased, there were tons of other options out there!

Preschool Spanish, French, Mandarin Chinese, Italian, and German were other no-gos. Liana can't even *say* her Rs, much less roll them. Plus, isn't this what *Dora* and *Kai Lan* are for?

As much as I think she could rock the cute outfit, Karate and Martial Arts just didn't seem like a good fit either. Personally I've found that whining is more effective at deterring bad guys (and good guys). I imagine her class Cobra Kai Dialogue going something like this:

"FEAR does not exist in this dojo DOES IT!?!"
"But whyyyyyy, Sensei?"

That brought me to my next discovery, Musical Theater. I like to get my *Jesus Christ Superstar* on just as much as the next girl, but I'm not sure if the world is ready for me to unleash mini Bernadette Peters on the world of pre-k just yet. This is mostly because when I say Bernadette Peters, I am thinking of a universe where B.P. has a voice that resembles a sick coyote yodeling.

I thought World Chefs might be a winner, because Liana likes helping in the kitchen. The intro read as follows: *"Children travel from the gardens of New Jersey to the coast of Italy cooking up wonderful new recipes along the way."* First of all, since when did the gardens of New Jersey mingle with the Italian coast in a culinary sentence? Second, do they know that my daughter's main ingredient in anything she "cooks" is her own saliva? I was pretty sure that she wasn't ready for public cooking yet.

It didn't take me long to cross Chess off my list. Sadly, Liana's only attempt at strategy thus far had been directing her smaller brother away from the tall towers she built using an irritating series of clicks and squeals. Based on my observations, Liana could search for Bobby Fisher, but she'd never find him.

Fairies and Friends was very intriguing! What little girl wouldn't like this class? I read with great interest until I got to this: *"Do you know how to catch fairies? Have you ever made a fairy house? Do you want to sprinkle fairy dust everywhere you go?"* Hold the front door. I have seventeen thousand Squinkies embedded in my shag carpet, and you want to encourage her to sprinkle fairy dust everywhere she goes? Pass.

My final strike out was Princesses and Superheroes. Before I could even think through the gender role questions I had about this one, I read this: *"...combines co-operative games, team building activities, literature, educational enrichment activities, and craft projects to ensure your powers will be supreme."* Umm … so now I'm wondering if the obsession I have with Princess Kate is due to her excessive crafting? And all this time I thought superheroes derived powers from their plastic underwear.

While she has yet to be enrolled in another Encore class, I am on the lookout, and if the situation gets desperate I may have to drop my standards. I'm sure I'll be able to find something if I keep looking. Will I choose wisely so Liana isn't sprinkling her fairy dust hither and yon, and driving me meatballs? YES SENSEI!

SUSAN LEE MACCARELLI writes primarily humor on her blog Pecked To Death By Chickens, though occasionally she'll reveal a soft underbelly—both in her writing, and by accident when bending over in the car to pick up a stray french fry off of the floor mats. Susan also helps other bloggers get featured on the websites they aspire to, via her blog resource site Beyond Your Blog. Features on sites like In the Powder Room, BlogHer, Mamapedia, Mamalode, Bonbon Break, and The Huffington Post help feed her attention-seeking behavior.

To the Rescue!
By Darcy Perdu
So Then Stories

I'm eager to ride some rides, but our kids spot yet *another* costumed Disney character, so they take off running toward her, their little autograph books flap-flap-flapping in their cute tiny hands.

Chloe, the three-year-old, shouts, "Sweeping Beauty! Sweeping Beauty!" as she trots alongside her five-year-old brother, Tucker, to join the long line of kids waiting to meet the princess.

I exchange a smile and a shrug with my husband, David, as we hustle to catch up.

"Who knew they'd be so obsessed to get autographs?" he asks. "This is their fourth one today!"

"Right?" I whisper. "We could've saved the Disneyland ticket price—and just invited the neighbors over dressed as princesses!"

The kids excitedly compare autographs in their books.

My energy's flagging, and the line's *at least* a half hour, so I motion over to a bench and tell the kids I'm going to catch a rest while they wait in line with Dad. David nods amiably since he snuck off for a latte during our *last* autograph session.

As I'm sitting there people-watching, I notice a little boy about two years old, walking along, looking distraught. I quickly survey the surrounding area for his family.

There are thousands of people at the park, of course, but none in the immediate vicinity seem to be attached to this kid.

Could ... *OMIGOD* ... could this be ... a LOST CHILD?

FANTASTIC!

Let me explain. I am a helper by nature. Holder of doors. Sharer of food. Dispenser of info. My whole life, I *love* helping people—especially strangers. Need directions? Of course! Lost your dog? Let's look! Can't figure out that spreadsheet? I'm your gal. The instant I board a bus or train, I immediately scan the crowd to see if there's someone more deserving of my seat. Old guy? Pregnant lady? Come on down! Flight attendant needs someone to squish in a middle seat so a mother and kid can sit together? No problem!

Nothing makes me happier than helping strangers. But I'm not altruistic by any means.

I just *love* that big grateful grin they give—or the look of relief—or the impressed nod.

Because, ya know, I'm an attention whore.

Over the years, I've occasionally seen a wandering kid that seemed like they *might* be lost, but the instant I think I'm about to make a child rescue, a parent or cousin or caretaker appears. And I'm always *devastated* at the lost opportunity to reunite a babe with his mama.

So basically, a *lost child* is my Holy Grail. My Big Foot. My White Whale.

Could this be it?

I quickly scan the crowd again—is there *anyone* here that looks like they might belong to this tyke? Nope. He's just walking right in front of me, directionless and distressed.

I jump into action! I carefully approach him, so as not to frighten my skittish little gazelle. "Honey? Are you O.K.? Is your Mom or Dad nearby?"

He hesitates and looks up to me, with a scrunched up face. He's not crying, but he looks *very* unhappy.

I repeat the question but he just stares at me blankly.

Oh. Maybe English is not his first language. He looks Hispanic, so maybe he speaks Spanish!

Excellent! I am *uniquely* qualified for this Rescue Mission!

My husband is half Hispanic and my kids are a quarter! (None of them actually *speaks* Spanish—but *no problema, chica*—I lived in Panama for three years as a child!)

I quickly try to remember my grade-school Spanish. I sputter, *"Hola! Como esta usted?"*

Omigod, I just asked him "How are you?" That's ridiculous. He is clearly *not* well.

Umm ... what else do I know how to say? Oh! Here ya go! I say, *"Donde esta Pedro? Pedro es en su casa!"*

The toddler looks at me curiously, like he's thinking, "Who the fuck is Pedro and why is he in my house?"

Oh, shit, oh, shit! I am *bungling* this! Other people are starting to notice me talking to this kid and I don't want them horning in on my rescue! I better pull it together if I want to keep the glory for myself.

I kneel down and say softly, *"Donde esta tu Mama, nino? Donde esta tu Papa?"*

His little face frowns, he looks around for them sadly, and shrugs.

"Oh, that's O.K., *nino*, we'll find them! Come with me to the store so we can tell the employees to help us, O.K.? Come over here, sweetie." He hesitates. *"Por favor, nino?"*

As I herd him toward the souvenir shop, I see David in the autograph line looking at me quizzically, like "What the hell are you doing? Where are you going? And don't you dare adopt a kid at this park. The two we have are exhausting enough!"

I smile wide and gesture excitedly, which just confuses him more.

As we walk to the store, I ask the toddler, *"Como se llama?"* but he's too shy to say his name. I dub him "Nino" in the meantime.

Someone asks me, "Is that kid lost?" Another says, "Is he O.K.?"

Back off, bitches. (I mean, please step away, well-meaning citizens.)

"Yes," I say authoritatively and self-importantly. "I'm reuniting him with his family."

The look impressed. *As they should.*

I hustle Nino into the shop and approach the cashier urgently. "This child is lost! We must find his family!"

I'm so excited, I'm shouting!

The cashier, on the other hand, is singularly unimpressed. She says, "O.K., I'll notify security." She's practically yawning as she places the call.

Omigod, girlie! Don't you see I'm making a CHILD RESCUE here? This is my big moment to shine!

She probably runs into lost kids all the time at a theme park, but this is my first time and I'm *milking* it, baby!

A guy pushing a stroller says, "I heard some mom down by the gift shop is looking for her kid." He points outside to an outdoor gift shop.

"Oh! Thank you!" I turn to the cashier and say, "That's probably his mom! I'll take him down there."

I reach to take the toddler's hand and the cashier says, "Nope."

Nope?

"Why not?"

"The safety protocol is to keep the child in one place; security will look for his family and bring them here or to the Lost Parents trailer," she says.

"But why not just take him to—"

"Nope. Security's on their way, ma'am. Thanks. We've got it from here."

Oh, not on my watch, lady! NOT ON MY WATCH!

Fine. If I can't bring Nino to the mountain, I'll bring the mountain to Nino!

I tell the toddler, "I'll be right back with your mama!"

I tear out of the shop, streaking past a puzzled David, run down the hill, and turn left into the outdoor shop. I frantically search the aisles, up and down—and then BAM! I see her! She's a young Hispanic woman with a diaper bag and no kid. She looks just as distressed as my little Nino.

I rush up to her. "Did you lose your son?"

"Si! Yes!" she says.

"I found him!" I shout exuberantly! "I found your son!"

She smiles wide with a huge look of relief. My heart soars.

"Come! Come with me! I know where he is! I'll take you to him!"

I turn to leave the shop and she follows me. I'm so excited, I can barely stand it!

I'm about to reunite a MOTHER with her CHILD! I am a HERO!

We dash out of the shop and run up the hill. I'm urging her along, "Come on, come on!" but I don't know if she speaks English, so I gesture a lot.

A gray-haired Hispanic lady joins us, holding another kid—she looks to be the grandma—and sure enough, my little mama greets her excitedly and points to me. They hug, but I'm all like "We ain't got time for this! We gotta get to the shop before Security takes your son to the Lost Parents trailer!"

I point to the souvenir shop up the hill and pick up the pace. "Come on, come on! It's up here! Hurry! Hurry!" I shout to them. They're running behind me—we're all puffing and panting— and *finally* we reach the top of the hill.

My little party breezes past David and the kids and Sweeping Beauty, and into the souvenir shop to my blasé cashier.

I'm practically out of breath.

"I ...[gasp for air] ... found the [take a breath] ... mom! I FOUND HER!!" I point at her, panting and gasping, "Here she is! We can reunite them! Where's her son?"

The cashier points at the grandma and says, "Right there."

WHAT?

I look closely at the grandma. She's about to keel over from all the running. She's holding a kid in her arms—but it's not Nino's <u>sibling</u>—it is NINO!

What the fuck?

Everybody's staring at me—the panting grandma, puzzled mama, sweet Nino, and the eye-rolling cashier.

She says, "Security found the grandma looking for the boy, so they let her bring him to the mom."

Grandma, Mama, and Nino all look at me.

I am speechless.

They are wondering why I brought them here.

The cashier asks, with that tone of voice you use when you ask a question that you *damn well* know the answer already: "Did you just run all the way *down* the hill to tell them the kid was here and then all of you ran *up* the hill—WITH THE KID?"

I spontaneously combust into a million tiny drops of humiliation and melt into the ground, never to be seen again.

I am *dying*.

Yes, yes, you officious little chick, that's EXACTLY what I did. In my feeble attempt for glory, I *interrupted* the reunion of the Mama and Grandma and Nino—and forced all of them to run up a hill to be *reunited with a kid they already had!*

Yep. Yeppers. Yeppadoody.

I shoot them a look like, "Well, why the hell were you following me if you already had the kid?" and they just looked at me with that sweet compliant expression that seemed to say, "Hey, if some crazy white lady starts yelling frantically for you to follow her quick quick hurry hurry in a language you don't speak well and she *insists* you follow her—well, *you follow her!*"

Oh my God.

I've never been so embarrassed in my life.

They probably thought they won a prize or something. And now here we are. No prize.

Mama and Grandma pat my arm and say, *"Gracias, gracias"* but I know Cashier Chick is gonna be laughin' it up in the Employee Lounge with Sweeping Beauty later tonight: "Omigod, Amy, you had to see this crusading woman trying to rescue a child that was *already* rescued! Bwahahaha!"

I trudge back over to the autograph line. The kids are almost to the front now.

David asks me, "What the hell was *that* all about?"

Oh my God, you guys. I couldn't tell him. *I COULD NOT TELL HIM.*

The Disneyland Debacle of the Thwarted Child Rescue Mission has remained Top Secret Classified Information...

Until now.

DARCY PERDU loves to pull up a bar stool and swap hilarious stories with friends about embarrassing kids, exasperating coworkers, vexing relationships, and the ever-perplexing public. Each story reminds someone else of a similar funny tale, so the laughter just keeps rolling. Darcy shares her bodacious blunders and funny stories at So Then Stories and invites you to share yours too! She won First Place in the 2014 National Society of Newspaper Columnists (Blogs under 100,000 monthly visits) as well as BlogHer Humor Voice of the Year Awards in 2013 & 2014. Follow her on Facebook, Twitter, and Pinterest.

Sometimes Drugs Are What You Need to
Get Through Motherhood. And That's Totally Okay.
By J.D. Bailey
Honest Mom

I'm going to tell you a story about the time I had a baby and thought I lost my mind. Not lost my mind as in, "Oh my God I'm so tired and have the worst mom-brain ever." No. I was truly afraid that I actually lost my mind and the essence of who I was. But don't worry! My story has a happy ending. I swear.

I'm telling you about this tough time in my life because it's the type of story that needs to be heard by more women. Too many moms have a baby and then are shocked to find they feel miserable. They hear other new moms talk about how hard this parenting gig is and nod along, but secretly wonder to themselves, *Do these women feel all the awful things I feel? Why am I so sad and angry about everything, when I'm supposed to be in love with being a mom? What in God's name is wrong with me?*

I'm here to tell you that if you have felt this way, you are absolutely not alone. And you're not a terrible person for having those feelings. Let me tell you how I found this out for myself.

One evening I came home after an unexpected spa-day treat from my husband. I had given birth about six weeks before to our second daughter. Hubby had noticed I was feeling really down and not like myself, so he thought maybe getting away for a little while would help. It was a blissful few hours. Even the car ride was euphoric. I hadn't been without a baby or a toddler clinging to me for weeks. As the masseuse rubbed away the knots in my back, I sighed a deep sigh I didn't realize I had in me.

When I got home, I opened the basement door and was assaulted by the sound of my infant wailing. My back muscles instantly reknotted. I could picture my baby's red face, her back arching, her complete misery and desperate need for me. But did I want to run to her and comfort her, like a good mother? No. I wanted to turn around and walk right back out the door. I wanted to jump back into my car and peel out of the neighborhood, driving as fast as I could, as far as I could, anywhere to escape the screaming child who was awaiting me.

And that's when I started to suspect that something was very wrong with me.

I wasn't always overwhelmed with these kinds of unmotherly feelings—in fact, when Grace was born I was filled with goofy, over-the-moon, new-mama feelings. The delivery was easy, I recovered quickly, and we spent three full days in the hospital together, snuggling and bonding. It was exactly the opposite of my first daughter's birth. It was amazing.

I remember happily gazing at Grace as she dozed on me after a nursing session, and thinking how much better this time around would be.

And things were good for a few weeks. I mean, I was horribly sleep-deprived and frazzled from dealing with my toddler, Anne, and a newborn. But that was to be expected.

What was not expected was how my brain would eventually betray me, filling me with extreme anger, sadness, anxiety, and a overwhelming sense of desperation.

The unwelcome feelings started to creep in slowly and surreptitiously, but then quickly got overwhelming. I started to resent my toddler's need for my attention and her temper tantrums. I got tired of my baby wanting to nurse all the time. I dreaded the frequent pumping to produce milk for bottles so my husband could do at least some nighttime feedings (Grace turned her nose up at formula). I got little enjoyment out of my day-to-day life. I was sad and angry and not myself at all. But I brushed those feelings aside and chalked them up to new-mom exhaustion. *It'll get better*, I told myself.

When I came home that evening from the spa and forced myself to go upstairs to deal with the screaming, I told myself that Grace just needed some mama snuggles. I could do this. It would be okay. Deep breaths. This is what good moms do.

I took Grace in my arms and snuggled her, and she desperately tried to latch onto my sweater. She was starving. I looked at my husband in horror—didn't he feed her while I was gone?

And then he delivered the news: Grace wouldn't take a bottle. At all. And she never took one again. From that moment on, I was destined to be her only source of food for months on end.

We tried every trick there was to get Grace to accept a bottle. We spent a fortune on weird bottles, glass bottles, and even a goofy-looking boob bottle that made my husband cringe. But Grace wouldn't go for it. She pursed her lips and turned her head, and would wail until I nursed her. I felt like she was punishing me for going to the spa that day. *Oh no you don't, Mama. You will never leave me again.*

To me, being my child's only source of nourishment was a prison sentence. I knew how often babies needed to eat, and I had a particularly voracious nurser on my hands. I would not be able to leave my house without my baby for months on end. Going out alone, being upstairs alone, and yes, even peeing alone … it all seemed unlikely to happen soon. Maybe ever again.

I felt trapped by my fussy and constantly nursing infant, who decided right then was also a perfect time to go through an epic bout of colic. I felt endless frustration and anger with my challenging toddler. I couldn't keep up with the laundry, the dishes, the cleaning up. I was overwhelmed, sad, anxious, and angry, every single day. I wondered if other moms felt as unmotherly as I felt. But I was afraid to ask.

And then one night, I lost it. I completely lost it on Anne while she was having a tantrum. I had had enough and I didn't know how I could possibly keep going. I remember the yellow walls of her room closing in on me, her red face screaming at me, my heart threatening to burst out of my chest. I was screaming and freaking out and thank God my husband was there. I felt completely powerless to stop what was happening to me.

When I eventually pulled myself together, I was humiliated, sick to my stomach, and desperately afraid. I knew I couldn't keep going like I was. Things were not going to just get better. This wasn't just a phase. I needed help.

So the next morning I called my OB/GYN and my primary care doc and uttered the words I was ashamed of and dreading to say: "I think I have postpartum depression." And boom. I was in the doc's office within hours, put on an antidepressant, and had a therapist appointment lined up for the next day.

Within days, I felt like myself again. Through the miracle of modern medicine and some kickin' therapy, perspective was bestowed upon me.

I was able to see this time as a phase. A difficult one, sure, especially for a person like me who craved some solitude each day and wasn't likely to get much of it. But I finally could understand that this time would end someday, and that helped me get through it—and eventually, even enjoy the little moments. I was also finally able to let more things go and not be so bothered by my messy house, my mismatched toddler, and my flabby postpartum body.

It was incredibly hard for me to admit I needed help, especially help in the form of drugs—something I had resisted at other tough points in my life. But I've learned that being a mom means doing hard things. And sometimes the hardest thing is accepting the help you need. Taking medication for postpartum depression was just like taking medication for any other medical condition, and there was nothing to be ashamed of. It took me a long time to be able to say that, but now I can.

Don't get me wrong. Things weren't perfect. But they were way more manageable. The everyday challenges of motherhood didn't seem so overwhelming. I felt *normal* again. I felt like *me* again. And it was glorious.

A few weeks later I was nursing Grace in the middle of the night. We were rocking in the glider in her tiny little room. Close, snuggling, connected once again. She reached up her tiny hand and planted it on my cheek, keeping her eyes locked on mine. I stared down at her with tears dropping down my cheeks as her tiny eyes spoke to me. *You're doing great, Mama. We're doing great.* And happily, finally, I knew she was right.

Honest Mom

JD BAILEY is the creator of the website and online community, Honest Mom. With candor and humor, JD writes to connect with other moms and raise awareness about women's mental health. Her writing has been featured in the original I Just Want to Pee Alone, *baystateparent magazine, The Huffington Post, and Scary Mommy. JD has been interviewed by Katie Couric about depression and anxiety in moms, and speaks at conferences such as BlogU. She's also a coffee-fueled, catnapping, slightly frazzled copywriter, social media manager, wife, and mom of two school-age girls.*

Open Letter to My Daughter:
My Mother was Right and You Should Think I Am, Too.
By Christine Burke
Keeper of The Fruit Loops

Dearest, Darlingest Daughter:

Today you rolled your eyes at me because I made you change your clothing before school. Somehow, the notion that a tank top and shorts on a January day was ~~a stupid idea~~ an inappropriate choice had escaped your nine-year-old mind. There was foot stomping (you), arguing (me) and a lot of attitude (all you, my dear drama queen).

You howled about "all the other girls" and "my favorite shirt."

You steadfastly maintained that you should be allowed to make your own choices. As your hazel eyes glared at me and your face shot me the "my mother is so lame" look, I realized that you aren't there yet. You couldn't see what I already know and you won't for many more years.

You *thought* you were right.

But I *knew* that I was.

Because here's the thing: your mother is always right and believe me, fewer sentences are harder to say out loud.

I know this because until recently, I couldn't admit it, either.

My mother has never worn denim. She has never said the F-word and has only missed Mass a handful of times in her almost seventy years on this planet. I've never seen her drink beer from a can, eat Chinese food, or entertain the idea of skydiving. She sends hand-written thank you notes for everything she receives and she remembers to buy birthday cards for everyone from her grandchildren to the mailman. She can tell you what Catholic feast day it is without having to consult a calendar.

In short, she's pretty much the exact opposite of me.

And for most of my teenage years and much of my adult life, I thought she was so completely wrong about Chinese food. And church. And about everything that goes into being a woman and a mother.

I didn't just think I was right. I *knew* I was.

Ahem. You can see where I'm going with this …

And, so because I want to save ~~myself years of arguing with you~~ you years of heartache, I decided to put a list together of all the ways I, er, *my mother*, was right.

Seven Reasons My Mother was Right (and I Am, Too)

1.) Living Away at College is a Must Because Your Mother Needs the Space.

If there was anything my mother was firm about, it was the fact that every child who passed through her womb was leaving the house when they turned eighteen. No exceptions. Period. If she was going to raise you, you were going to leave her to see the big scary world beyond her kitchen. She was fond of saying "You raise children to leave you" and she planted the seeds in our head fairly early on that we were expected to get the hell out of Dodge and make something of ourselves. She was NOT paying our bills when we were forty.

(Note: I suspect this dogma was put in place because after three kids, seven interstate moves and a husband who traveled thirty weeks of the year, she wanted some peace and freaking quiet. She's a patient woman and was willing to wait until that last kid left to finally hear herself think.)

Darling Daughter, you WILL be living in a dorm when it comes time. Because my mother was right and I am, too. And because I need some time to think.

2.) Always Start at the Clearance Rack. Always.

Before Macklemore and Ryan made poppin' tags a "thing," my mother was cruising the clearance racks and clipping coupons. "Buy One, Get One Free" was her anthem, her motto. We'd walk into the store and she'd dive for the fifty percent off rack. And it drove me nuts. I used to roll my eyes inwardly because I wanted, just once, to buy one of the pretty items displayed at the front of the store. Just once, I wanted to not shop in the bowels of a department store, near the service exit. And, for the love of all that was holy, I couldn't stand the store brand fruit loops bought with a coupon. Name brand, baby!

But, as I found out about thirty seconds after leaving home, life ain't cheap. And, your standards change very quickly when it's your own green that's leaving your pocket to pay for the stuff you buy. The day I realized I only had enough in my bank account to buy a box of rice, some pasta sauce, and a head of lettuce was the day I was grateful that my mom had taught me how to stretch a dollar. I ate Spanish rice and salad that night and though it wasn't fancy, I'd paid for it on my own.

Darling Daughter, it's okay to have expensive tastes. Go ahead. Buy those Louboutins. But, with a coupon, at a seventy-five percent off sale AFTER they've already been marked down. Better yet, be happy with the Kohl's knockoffs.

3.) Graciousness Matters. A Lot.

My mother is the Thank You Note Queen. If you give her a gift, she writes you a note in proper English with sentences that can be diagrammed. Her punctuation is impeccable and she always uses the three paragraph rule to state her thoughts. I can remember being eight years old and sitting at the kitchen table long into the evening writing thank you notes after my First Communion. Verbal thank yous were a no-go in our house. You said thank you in the form of creamy white cardstock, black pen, and a stamped envelope.

Darling Daughter: A heartfelt, gracious thank you goes a long way. Learn it. And do it because I said so. And so does your grandmother. You'll thank us, I promise.

4.) There is No Excuse for Bad Hair. Ever.

In the seventies, women got their hair frosted by a beautician in a *Steel Magnolias*-type salon. My mom would go to the hairdresser religiously to get her hairs did and done up. She had three young kids, a husband who traveled, and often lived in a city where she didn't have family to help out. She'd hire a babysitter if she could, but, more often than not, she'd drag us with her so she could hide her gray hair. When her hair was again youthful and beautifully coiffed, she'd take us home with a little bit of a spring in her step. It was evident her lovely hair made her feel better about driving a green Ford Grenada in Candies sandals with three kids rolling around in the backseat.

When I was a new mom and money was tight, my mother always put her foot down when it came to where I skimped money. A good haircut or color was a priority for sanity and it was non-negotiable. Sometimes, in those early, sleep deprived years, she'd slip me a little extra money so I could pamper myself. Whether it was a manicure or a good haircut, her message was clear: take care of yourself so you can take care of them.

Darling Daughter: Make the time for yourself because you are worth the extra money. Your children need to see you put yourself first. It is not selfish to want to be away from the chaos and demands of motherhood. And, your mother will always slip you a twenty so you can do your roots ...

5.) You Can Count Your Good Friends on Your Left Hand.

Let's face it: girls are downright mean. From little snots on the playground to teenage bullies to snarky moms, women be haters. And it's hard, really hard, when you are the girl who wants to play nice with everyone. No matter your age, there's always going to be that group of women who are popular, pretty, and pretentious and who make sure you know their group is clooooosed to new members.

When I was in fifth grade, I was invited to a sleepover birthday party and the snotty birthday girl made sure to let everyone know she only invited me because her mother made her. While I was devastated, my mother was just plain pissed. PISSED. Hell hath no fury like a mother scorned, I tell you. She piled me into the car, birthday present and all, and together, we dropped the present off with our re-grets that I couldn't stay. And, when my mother looked her mother in the eye and said, "She has better things to do than play with your daughter," I learned to hold my head high in my Benetton sweater and stand my ground with Mean Girls. I also learned not to mess with my mother.

So, I want you to put this book down right now and take a good look at your left hand. See those five fingers? Each one will have a name attached to it, the name of a friend who will get out of bed to bail you out of jail, meet you at the hospital, or carry the baseball bat to an ex-boyfriend's car with you. Your Left Hand Friends are the ones that matter.

Darling Daughter: Let the haters hate because your Left Hand Friends ain't got time for that …

6.) Your Kids Don't Always do What is Expected. But Moms Love You Anyway.

When you bring a tiny bundle home from the hospital, parents are filled with expectations and dreams. Will Little Johnny cure can-cer? Will Little Suzy be an Olympic athlete? You stare into that tiny face and, even though you aren't supposed to, you dream big. Huge.

Then Little Johnny decides to go and become a professional beach bum. Little Suzy runs off to the circus and only calls on Christ-mas to talk about her new husband, the lion tamer. Though beach lounging and tight rope walking aren't what you had planned, you realize that if your kids are happy, so are you. And, you will always read your kid's blogs, even the ones with "earthy" language. Because I'm happy and you're proud, right, Mom?

Darling Daughter: Go ahead. Join the circus and I'll be in the front row, cheering your juggling routine. But you better ass be able to pay your bills. See number one. Ahem.

7.) Daughters Make You Brave.

Every day, I think about the fact that you are watching me, looking to me to show you the ropes. When you run to my room at night after a nightmare or need me to push you higher on the swings, I know you need me to help you to be brave. With every skinned knee, heartache, and disappointment you lay at my feet, I am ever conscious that you need to learn from me.

But, the real truth is that you, my Darling Daughter, are the one who makes me a braver woman. I face my fears every day, from getting onto the scary chair lift at the ski resort to putting my words on paper for the world to critique. Not because I want praise. Not because I want to be famous. But because, when I look into your eyes, I want you to look back at a woman who makes you proud.

Darling Daughter: I am brave because you are my daughter. But I'll always think the ski lift is scary.

My mother was right. Well, except for Chinese food. Because egg rolls. I steadfastly maintain that she's missing out on culinary nirvana, but I digress. She's been right all these years and has been gracious enough to hide her laughter behind my back. She's let me grow and come to this realization on my own as all good mothers do.

And, Darling Daughter, if someday, you'd like to quietly whisper in my ear, "You were right, Mom," I promise I won't say, "I told you so."

I'll think it, though.

Ahem.

With love,

Your Mother

I Still Just Want to Pee Alone

CHRISTINE BURKE is the Keeper of the Fruit Loops, Manager of the Fecal Roster and Driver of the People Mover. In other words, she's a mom. An Erma Bombeck Martha Stewart with a Roseanne Barr twist, she has the mouth and organized cabinets to prove it. She resides in Pennsylvania with her ever budget conscious husband, two blog inspiring Fruit Loops and her extensive collection of thrift shop shoes. In her spare time, she runs marathons, governs the PTA like nobody's business and drinks cheap wine to cope with it all. Her personal blog is Keeper of the Fruit Loops.

How the Mighty Have Fallen
(and by "Mighty" I Mean "Boobs")
By Rita Templeton
Fighting off Frumpy

From the minute the two lines appeared on the pregnancy test, heralding the arrival of my first little money-sucker—er, baby—I made it my sole mission to be completely prepared. I devoured book after book like I was being paid to process the information. If someone had given me a pop quiz about what to pack in the perfect hospital bag or what a newborn's first poop was made of, I'd have yawned and asked if they had any harder questions.

But you know what all the literature—at least the kind I read—failed to mention? Exactly how much pregnancy (and especially multiple pregnancies) will jack your shit *up*.

I'm not talking about the stuff immediately following birth. We all know about the floppy, bread-dough belly, the leaky boobs, and the poor beaten-up postpartum vagina. I'm talking about later on down the line: horrifying, permanent changes that you will bemoan long after your sweet newborn baby has turned into a nose-picking kid.

I never had a swimsuit-model bod or anything like that, and nobody has ever thrown money at a plastic surgeon to procure exact replicas of my unimpressive B-cups. Prior to pregnancy, though, I still looked pretty decent by most standards. So the cosmos were like, "Ha! You've spent your life being cute, now let's see how you deal with being the most hideous pregnant woman ever to waddle the earth!" Right then, I was bitch-slapped with an astonishing ninety pound weight gain—which led, of course, to enough extra skin to upholster a couch. (A *striped* couch, because holy stretch marks!) But that wasn't even the surprise.

Seeing as the rest of me was expanding by leaps and bounds, my feet decided to join the party. Did you know that pregnancy could make your feet bigger? Yeah, me neither—until mine went from a respectable size nine to a much less attractive size clown-shoe, and stayed that way. I still can't buy certain styles, because shoes that look super cute on regular-sized feet look like pontoon boats on mine. I may as well tromp around in cereal boxes.

I can deal with bigger feet (not like I have much of a choice), but I'm pretty disheartened at the wider hips that also seem to be an enduring part of the pregnancy package. With each baby, my body has reshaped itself. And it's not a matter of extra weight: even in the times when I'm back down to my pre-pregnancy poundage (or, you know, close enough), I still can't come close to fitting into any of my old jeans. I guess that's what people mean when they refer to "child-bearing hips," but if that's the case, I look like I've birthed twenty sets of twins. Pear-shaped is my reality now. It's not fair.

And my boobs. *My boobs.* Back in the days when Pamela Anderson was *Baywatch*-ing it up and down the beach, nearly spilling out the top of her red swimsuit, I was a flat-chested teenager lamenting regularly to my mother about my lack of cleavage. "But honey," my similarly flat-chested mom would say, "when they're small, they don't sag."

LIES.

I mean, I should have known that was a gross untruth, coming from the lady who told me that Santa Claus and the Tooth Fairy were real. But I optimistically believed her. It was my one beacon of hope: even if big, jiggling *Baywatch* titties weren't in my future, they'd still be perky later on! I'd have the last laugh! However, pregnancy and nursing made them (temporarily) bigger—and then when they weren't needed for practical purposes any more, they cruelly deflated. Now it's like they've given up; their pride is gone, and they point tiredly toward my belly button, like oranges in an old pair of tube socks.

Okay, *plums* in old tube socks. Geez.

And as if all these bodily changes weren't enough of a travesty? Like some sort of weird hormonal joke, I grew a beard. Not a few rogue chin hairs, but a smattering of stubbly growth that extends down my neck and threatens my very femininity. I've resigned myself to the fact that now—and for the rest of my freaking life—I will require an arsenal of depilatories and razors and wax strips to tame my manly thatch of chin-pubes. With each pregnancy comes a few more hairs, a few more reminders that *I never read about in any of the books.* The beard, the big feet, the wider hips, the chronically-depressed boobs—those weren't mentioned among the pages I so eagerly devoured.

Perhaps these things are deliberately left out. Maybe the authors figure that we're going to be so overwhelmed at the prospect of passing a human being through our nether-regions—and the immediate consequences—that they just can't bear to tell us that we're *also* going to sprout a goatee or sport exercise-resistant saddlebags. But it's, you know, pretty useful information.

Maybe instead of including it in books for moms-to-be, they should just start casually slipping this info into teen pregnancy prevention literature. I bet the rates would plummet. Like my boobs.

You can find RITA TEMPLETON (and her band of rogue chin hairs) blogging at Fighting off Frumpy, where she writes about the challenges of raising four boys while trying to retain at least a little shred of girlishness. She is a regular contributor to Scary Mommy, and has been featured on The Huffington Post and HuffPost Live. Rita lives in Davenport, Iowa with her husband, their sons, and a menagerie of spoiled pets. When she isn't writing, she's either baking, cleaning up a heinous mess, or looking for a supportive bra.

Let's Piss-Off the Babies
By Nicole Leigh Shaw
Nicole Leigh Shaw, Tyop Aretist

There's been a lot of lip service paid to the topic of managing baby jerkiness. There are dissertations on swaddling, soothing, and calming our tiniest humans. Veteran moms tell new moms the tips and tricks that worked for them. New moms take notes from parenting books, laminate them, and hang them on the nursery door in the hopes that they've stumbled upon the formula for success.

It's all stuff and nonsense. Babies are just jerks. There's only one rule the first year of their life. Survive. You'll need to learn how to stay alive on cold coffee and Netflix for that first year if you have any hope of weathering the sheer cheekiness of the toddler stage.

That's long been the party line. Just get through it. This too shall pass. They are only little, after all. We've all been there.

But I say gritting our teeth and bearing down during these early years isn't enough. It's time for revenge. It's time to tell these babies and toddlers where to stick their pouty faces.

"But my baby isn't a jerk!" you say. Does your baby:

- Wake you multiple times in the night to satisfy his own selfish needs?
- Have no problem abruptly ending your social outing by doing objectionable things in public like, but not limited to, pooping liquid fire up and out the back of her diaper?
- Have the nerve to foul you're going-out t-shirt with spit up, a move that would earn any other human a face slap?

If you answered "yes" to any of these scenarios, your baby is a jerk.

It's probably (but not necessarily) true that your baby just doesn't know any better. Or it's possible that you're being played. Damn it if my daughter didn't once poke me in the eye five consecutive times when she was about seven months old and I was wearing mascara for the first time in months. This made my eye water and my mascara run and tell me, I dare you, that she didn't have an agenda. Tell me to my mascara-lined face.

Nicole Leigh Shaw, Tyop Aretist

What else can we call a human who refuses to keep socks on in the dead of winter, pulling them off or kicking feet so furiously that hours pass and you find yourself asking an unintelligible two-month-old, "Where the loving hell did your sock go?" Do you call her willful? Do you make excuses like, "She's nine weeks old"? Or is the hard truth that she's a real Dick Richard?

I've met a lot of raging jackholes in my day, and the thing they most powerfully remind me of are babies. Drunk guy at the party with the puke on the front of his shirt? What a juvenile. Lady crying because her latte wasn't nonfat? Such a child. In fact, we say that, don't we? When adults or adolescents act the fool we say, "You're being such a *baby*." Baby, baby, stick your head in gravy. Babies are shitbirds.

Why, I once knew a baby that cave painted her walls and crib with her own feces. That baby was me and I was a real piece of work. If I did that in my marital bed it would be grounds for divorce. It would be good reason for a legally binding absolution of my marriage.

But babies are like unarmed miscreants, trying to hustle you with only their bare knuckles to back up their threats. It's toddlers who bring the big guns to the knife fight. And what are you holding, parents? A Nerf gun without bullets.

Are we just going to sit here and take it? Are we really going to plod along as we have for the history of humankind and placate these petulant ne'er-do-wells? Or are we going to revolt against the jerk babies and jerk toddlers of the world and say, "It doesn't look like I will ever make you happy, so I'm done trying. You think you've got something to cry about? Well you've got another think coming!"

Radical thought: Let's stop trying to make them happy and start actively trying to piss them off. No longer will we labor in a world where crying babies are shushed and soothed, whooshing slowly back and forth in the baby swing it took us twenty-three straight minutes to adjust to the perfect speed so that this whining, wild-eyed crier would finally drift off long enough for us to poop—*and wipe*.

I Still Just Want to Pee Alone

Let's crank that swing up to ten and laugh while they wail. Oh, you no likely the zippy-zippy swing time? Well, we don't like stringing together four hours of sleep in seven-minute intervals.

Got a baby who only likes one pacifier, but only when you hold it in his mouth for fifteen minutes until you're sure it's safe to move your hand away? Burn it. Melt that plastic shackle right in front of his wittle eyes and swallow the molten cocktail in one gulp because you are one crazy son of a mother and you've had just about enough of this crap.

Does your toddler have a problem with the color yellow? Is it the one and only color that throws him into a blind rage during which he refuses sustenance, entertainment, and comfort? Guess what, you tyrannical ingrate? All the yellow things shall be yours. Yellow sippy cups and yellow balloons and a fuzzy yellow blanket that mommy will keep laying across your legs in the stroller while you protest because mommy can and because the five-point harness says you'll just sit there and take it.

Are there thirty-five hours of Nick Jr., Disney Junior, and PBS Kids taking up space on your DVR because a certain three-foot-tall despot demands MORE CAILLOU? End her world—delete it all. Delete it all while she looks on and then make her sit through a binge season of *The Bachelor*. Who's the despot now, changeling?

But damn if it isn't actually easier than all that. We are, after all, talking about babies and toddlers, the most taciturn creatures on the planet. Why, I've seen a toddler get *exactly what she asked for* and still launch a twenty-minute oration on the benefits of screaming. Why start with the nuclear threats when we can launch our campaign with these simple but effective strategies?

Here are fifty surefire ways to piss off babies and toddlers:
1. Swaddle them.
2. Don't swaddle them.
3. Stop holding them.
4. Go out with them in public.
5. Try something new.
6. Bathe them.

7. Bathe yourself.
8. Feed them.
9. Don't feed them.
10. Buy the wrong snacks.
11. Have a conversation with another adult.
12. Sleep when they sleep.
13. Wipe their snotty noses.
14. Pay attention to another child.
15. Tell them "No."
16. Tell them "Yes."
17. Tell them it's nap time.
18. Help them with something.
19. Don't help them with something.
20. Stop driving, strolling, or bouncing them.
21. Eat a hot meal.
22. Enjoy a book.
23. Sit down.
24. Stop watching them when they say "Watch me!"
25. Have another baby.
26. Take them for professional photos.
27. Make them take turns.
28. Suggest something reasonable and sane.
29. Clip their fingernails.
30. Leave the room.
31. Give them a cupcake with too much frosting.
32. Give them a cupcake with too little frosting.
33. Fail to grasp what the correct cupcake to frosting ratio is because it's all really just a huge mind screw.
34. Try to clean under their neck folds.
35. Don't let them pull your hair.
36. Don't let them put their fingers in your mouth.
37. Don't let them eat mulch.
38. Be unable to make things that will happen tomorrow, happen today.
39. Brush their hair.

40. Brush their teeth.
41. Tell them when they are wearing an article of clothing backwards.
42. Plan something in advance.
43. Change your appearance with a haircut or a shave.
44. Skip a page in a book they clearly aren't listening to.
45. Change a full diaper.
46. Don't change a full diaper.
47. Make them wear shoes.
48. Make them wear pants.
49. Make yourself happy.
50. Have a life.

We can do this. Why wait until they are teens to take our revenge, singing along to pop songs on the radio while carpooling their friends about town? Let's make their world a living hell right this minute. Any good bully knows that it's easiest to pick on smaller people. Why wait for wee ones to grow-up when we can eat their fruit snacks—every last packet—right in front of them this very minute?

Be the change you want to see in the world, parents. There are enough babies and toddlers running us around on their invisible leashes, binding us to their whims with legal responsibility for their care and safety. It's our turn to put the leash on them. It's our turn to be the parents in the airport dragging a sobbing sack of humanity behind us on a puppy-themed harness, calling back over our shoulder, "No Flamin' Hot Cheetos for you because you're two and you have no idea what you're asking for. So cry and kick but suck it up, Sunshine. There's a new sheriff in town. And *she* eats the Flamin' Hot Cheetos around here."

All four of NICOLE LEIGH SHAW's kids are still breathing. Award, please. She blogs at NicoleLeighShaw.com where she's embarrassed her mother many, many times.

A Day with MY Niece
By Tracy Sano
Tracy on the Rocks

My niece and I have always had a special relationship. Even though I live across the country, my sister has made a point from the time she was born to make sure little Kailee knew her auntie. She would send me pictures of the baby with a photo of me with her so we could be together from far away. It wasn't just that we talked and Skyped and sent packages though—there was something more than that. When people saw Kailee, they would always tell me, "My God! If I didn't know she was your sister's kid, I'd be convinced she was yours! She looks like you, she talks like you ... she's sassy like you—even her mannerisms are like yours!"

Whenever Kailee is giving my sister a run for her money (which is often...she's just like me, remember?), my sister Mandy will text me and say, "YOUR niece is being very naughty" or "YOUR niece is three seconds away from going into time out for the rest of her life." When she's being a pain in the butt, she's MY niece.

Last year, when my sister was due to have Baby Number Two, I planned to stay with them for a few weeks to help around the house and make sure Kailee's transition to going from center-of-attention to big sister went smoothly. Kailee was three and by now, she knew how to play Auntie like fiddle.

Let me give you an example of her fiddle-playing: I had given her the book, *If You Give a Mouse a Cookie* last time I was visiting. Kailee loved that book and I must have read it to her a million times—minimum. I even bought myself a copy so I could read it to her over Skype. One day when my sister and I were talking on the phone, Kailee grabbed it from her in a panic, "Auntie! I can't find the cookie book!" she exclaimed.

"O.K., Sweetheart. I can send you a new book."

Mandy snatched the phone away from her and scolded her, "Kailee! You haven't even LOOKED for the cookie book. It's probably upstairs with your other books!"

To me, she said, "Do NOT let that kid con you into sending her things!"

I Still Just Want to Pee Alone

A few weeks later, we were Facetiming. Kailee took the iPad and brought me into her room-without her mom. She looked around. She looked around again. When she determined the coast was clear, she turned her attention back to me and she whispered, "Auntie, I still can't find the cookie book."

Just as I was promising her a new one, my sister walked into the room. "Is YOUR niece trying to con you into buying her a new book again?" I put my head down like we had both just gotten in trouble.

So you see, Kailee was no stranger to the Auntie Game and by the time I made my way out to see them for my nephew Lucas' arrival, I was armed with the knowledge that she had me wrapped around her finger. And to be honest, I loved it. I live far away. I WANT to be the fun auntie, the one who spoils her and who she gets excited to see. I ate it up.

My three week visit was one of the best times of my life. I got to bond with my sister and her family in a way I couldn't with just a long weekend trip. Baby Lucas was an amazing addition to our family and Kailee and I picked right up where we had left off. I adored her and she adored me. As much as she knew she could jump all over me and get me to do whatever she wanted, she knew the rules too. When I woke up in the wee early morning hours to go to the bathroom, I would trip over her little body, curled up outside my room with a blanket she had yanked off of her bed, waiting for me to wake up. She knew better than to wake up the Morning Auntie Beast.

Kailee and I were best buds. She wanted to do everything I did. When I would set up my laptop to get some work done, she would sit down right next to me scribbling on a piece of "important paper" as she called it, or with the family iPad. One day I was sitting there working and all of a sudden, my sister's face via Skype popped up on my screen. Looking over at Kailee, sitting on the stool next to me, I asked, "Kailee? Are you trying to Skype me?"

"Yes, Auntie," she giggled.

"But Kailee, I'm sitting right *next* to you ..."

"O.K., then you go in the dining room and pretend we're far away," she replied.

"Umm, no. I'm working. *You* go in the other room and we can Skype and pretend we're far away." And so we did.

My sister came downstairs from putting the baby down for a nap. "Hey, are you two knuckleheads Skyping each other in the same house?" she asked, shaking her head.

Kailee and I burst out laughing. "YES!" as we looked at each other on the Skype screen in hysterics.

My sister had scheduled a newborn photo shoot for Lucas with her photographer for the next day. She wanted to get some photos with Kailee too, but I was going to take her on a special Auntie/Kailee date after they got some shots with her in them, so she wouldn't get bored or be in the way. I was excited to take Kailee all on my own. I envisioned a special day that she would remember when she got older. I'll admit, I was also a little excited to show my younger sister—who always seemed to be able to juggle it all—that her older, non-parent sister could handle it. How hard could it be, anyway? Kailee and I were besties, after all.

I showed up at the photographer's studio the next day ready to take Kailee out for ice cream. We were going to go to Friendly's, a family-friendly ice cream parlor and restaurant I used to love going to when I was a kid. Kailee was in a beautiful purple chiffon dress and looked like a pretty little three-year-old angel. "Come on, Kailee." I reached for her hand as I finished packing up her backpack.

Without warning, the little angelic face contorted into a crying, sniffling, wailing mess. "I don't wanna leave, I wanna stay here with Mommy!!!!!" she cried.

"Umm. Yes, but sweetheart, we're going to get ICE CREAM!" I told her, excitedly. Why the hell was she *crying*? She was all dressed up with somewhere to go. Why would she want to hang around here when she was going somewhere awesome ... and with *me*? I couldn't make sense of it.

The crying didn't stop as I led her to the car. I put the sniffling child into her car seat and fumbled with the bazillion straps and buckles. Through sniffling and crying she pointed out that I was buckling her all wrong and helped me get it right. I already felt like a failure.

I got into the front seat and cheerily began talking about ice cream. "Kailee, what flavor are you going to get? I love chocolate! Will you get sprinkles on yours?" Kailee ate her peanut butter and jelly sandwich my sister had packed for her and started to cheer up with all the ice cream talk. We chatted about strawberry ice cream the entire way to Friendly's.

When we walked into the restaurant, the hostess greeted us. "I want strawberry!" Kailee announced. She looked up at me and added, "Please!" The hostess laughed as she led us to our table and told us we had to tell our waitress about the strawberry ice cream. Our server came a few minutes later. Kailee was trying to hard to be patient, but how many people did she have to tell about the strawberry ice cream? "I want strawberry ice cream—*please!*" Kailee told the waitress. I ordered a salad.

"Auntie, are you getting strawberry ice cream too?" she asked.

"No, sweetheart, I haven't eaten lunch yet so I'm just going to get a boring salad. But since you ate your peanut butter sandwich, you get to have dessert."

When the waitress came by to check on us a few minutes later, Kailee made her giggle when she asked her, "Are you still making Auntie's BORING salad?" Once the boring salad and the strawberry ice cream came out, the meltdown from earlier was forgotten. Kailee was pretending her spoon was stuck in the ice cream like the Sword in the Stone and we were chatting and laughing like the best friends that we were. Then Kailee abruptly dropped her spoon on the table mid-"sword" removal. "I have to poop," she declared.

O.K. The kid had to poop. Was I supposed to just leave our food on the table? Should I tell the waitress we'd be right back? Was it O.K to just leave our coats in the booth? Nobody would roofie us in a Friendly's, right? I grabbed my purse and took her hand and led her to the Ladies' Room. I carefully laid down a wax seat-cover and as I lifted her tiny body onto the toilet, I couldn't help but notice how enormous it looked with her sitting on it. I was so afraid she was going to fall in. How would she keep her balance without touching the toilet?

AHH!! I got my answer as she grabbed the sides of the toilet to hold herself up! Sick! Who *knows* when the last time that thing got cleaned? Gross, gross, gross! O.K., I would just make sure I washed her hands really well. No big deal. She finished up and then I figured while we were in there, I should go too. I was mid-stream when Kailee ran over to the door and whipped it open so all of the diners sitting outside the bathroom got a great view of Auntie on the can. "Kailee! Please close the door!" I pleaded with her, as an eighty-year-old man with age spots all over his head waved at me. I waved back at him in defeat.

After I finished, I lifted her up and helped her wash her hands. When I put her back down, I looked at her sternly, glancing at the toilet shuddering and said, "Kailee, do not touch ANYTHING, O.K.?" and then I leaned over the sink to wash my own hands. As I reached for a paper towel, I caught a glimpse of Kailee out of the corner of my eye. There she stood, in her purple chiffon dress, with strawberry ice cream dripped on the front and one finger pointedly on the toilet seat while she looked up at me with a big grin of defiance.

"You little—!" I couldn't help but laugh as I grabbed her and lifted her up *again* to wash her hands. What a little shit!

With the bathroom debacle behind us, we headed back to our booth. We finished up our food and bundled up in our coats and mittens. As we approached the door, the woman at the hostess stand asked us if we wanted a balloon. Kailee's face lit up when the hostess handed her a pink balloon. You would have thought Kailee had just won the Kid's Lottery. The balloon was attached to a little stick. Kailee was twirling it around everywhere. Back in the car, (this time I did much better with her straps and buckles, she only had to help me a little bit) she discovered she could reach Auntie with the balloon on a stick and thought it was just hilarious to whack me with it over and over from the backseat. "Kailee, please don't hit Auntie with the balloon. First of all, it's dangerous while I try to drive. Also, you don't want your balloon to pop, do you?"

Whelp. No sooner had I gotten the words out did I hear POP!

From there, everything was a blur. The meltdown of all meltdowns ensued. "Kailee, we can get you a new balloon. We'll get you a new balloon soon, I promise. Sweetheart, if you stop crying, I'll stop at the first store that sells balloons," I desperately pleaded with her to no avail.

"I. Want. [hiccup] That. Balloon. Please fix my balloon for me, Auntie. Please, Auntie, please fix it. Please make it not be broken, Auntie. Auntie, fix it. *Pleeeeeease,*" she sobbed.

My heart broke a little bit that day; it was the first time I wasn't able to fix something for Kailee, to make her happy. Not for the first time that day, I felt like a failure.

We finally got back to the house and Kailee carried the stick with the deflated balloon remnants dangling from it in defeat. "Kailee, do you want to do an art project, Sweetheart?"

"No, Auntie. I had a long day. I think I'll take a rest." (She was too big for naps, of course. But rests were O.K.)

"You know what, K? That sounds like a wonderful idea." I snuggled up next to her and read her the cookie book. We had finally "found it" up in her bookshelf.

My sister came home shortly after. "So how did it go?" she asked when she saw the two of us curled up together.

"Well, let me tell you: YOUR daughter—" I stopped myself and grinned down at my best bud and corrected myself. "You know what? MY niece and I had a great day together."

TRACY SANO has always loved telling funny stories and she currently logs her rants on her humor blog, Tracy on the Rocks. She has an unhealthy obsession with firefighters, hotdogs, and anything pink. Tracy's favorite thing to do—besides drink wine—is laugh until her stomach hurts (which doesn't take much, considering how much she also hates working out). Her biggest accomplishment to date is being named the World's Best Auntie, by those who matter.
Check out her blog or follow her on Twitter.

The Library Mom
By Janel Mills
649.133: Girls, the Care and Maintenance Of.

I have worked in college libraries since I was twenty-three years old. At the beginning of my career, I was pretty close to the same age as a lot of the college students who visited my library. When they used slang, I immediately knew what they meant. Sometimes I would see a student wearing a skirt that I had just bought the previous weekend at the mall. We drove the same piece of shit cars to campus. I was young, cool, and childless. Once, as a campus event, I brought in my video game system and set it up in the student lounge, offering to play *Guitar Hero* with students during breaks between classes. I spent the day destroying most of the students that took me up on my offer, because I would sit at home for hours late at night learning how to beat "Crazy Train" on expert mode. Nobody came to me for advice on anything except their APA style formatting, and I liked it that way. I went to library school to become a *librarian*, not a fucking life coach. If anyone came to me crying, I hauled their ass down to the student counselor with a concerned smile and a shoulder squeeze. There, there. Now, if you'll excuse me, I'll just be on my way back to my safe, orderly library, where I will order books on legalizing marijuana and assisted suicide and every other "controversial" topic that you freshmen English students just *love* to write about.

Nowadays, it's a completely different story. I'm not really old, per se, but I am just old enough that I don't understand slang until it's been around long enough to make it into a Buzzfeed list, and I don't fit into any of the skirts I bought at the mall ten years ago (which, incidentally, is the last time I went shopping by myself at the mall). I recently traded in the piece of shit car that let me blend in with the student body for a sweet minivan. I haven't played *Guitar Hero* in years, and I'm not even really sure which corner of the family room we shoved the guitars. I'm just old enough that I could be the mother of most of the freshmen that wander through our doors (if my high school experience had been a little bit different).

All too often, I find myself accidentally acting like I *am* their mothers. Once, while sitting at the front desk, a student approached me and asked for a Band-Aid. She had short cropped hair that was dyed a beautiful shade of "Fuck *you*, Mom!" purple. If she were more than eighteen years old, I will gladly give you the *Dookie* CD I was probably listening to the day she was born. The X-Acto knife she had been using to trim and mount her art project had slipped and sliced her finger open, and it started to bleed. The combination of her hair, her age, and the blood flipped a switch in my head. I reached into the desk drawer and pulled out a Band-Aid. Instead of handing it to her to put on her own finger like the quasi-adult that she was, I took it out of the wrapper. I was already holding the ends of the Band-Aid and reaching out to apply it to her boo-boo when I looked up and saw her horrified face. Sheepishly, I handed her the Band-Aid. I tried to resist telling her she should be careful, that she may need stitches, but I think you and I both know that I couldn't stop myself. I did, however, resist the urge to offer to kiss it and make it better because I still enjoy being employed.

While this girl definitely felt like she was above having her boo-boo fixed for her, there are times when it becomes painfully clear that many of these kids need someone to mom the fuck out on them. For example, there was the time my student assistant came to work with an itchy full-body rash. He was having an allergic reaction to some crazy body-building supplement he drank the day before. Within the first hour of his shift, he went from itchy to OMG CAN'T STOP WON'T STOP ITCHING. Since I couldn't help but notice the bright red guy frantically scratching his arms and pacing back and forth behind my circulation desk, I asked him if he was okay.

"No! I can't stop itching! I brought some Benadryl to work with me, and I think I'm going to take some."

The look in this kid's eye got me to pay attention to the mom alarm bells already jangling in my head. "How much Benadryl are you planning on taking?"

"I'm just going to take three or four. I'm so itchy!"

Oh shit. "Bring me the box."

As it turns out, my loveable genius of a lunkhead was planning on taking three to four *times* the amount of Benadryl he should have taken. He was then planning on curling up and taking a nap in his car. Forever, apparently, but not on purpose. He needed a mom to step in and let him know that hey, buddy, maybe it would be wise to read the dosage instructions before taking medication instead of just guesstimating. It is days like these that I wish I could call up these kids' parents and let them know that someone else is on duty on their behalf. "Hey, Ms. Jorgenson. Please don't worry about Josh. I've got this under control over here. Carry on."

Because that's who I have become. I am no longer the campus librarian. I am now the library mom. I nurse them through break-ups, cheer for them when they pass their exams, and, when necessary, tell them to get out of my office and go do their goddamn homework *now*, not in five minutes, not after watching one more YouTube video, but RIGHT NOW. I've also been known to shift my voice into a certain tone—*you* know the tone I'm talking about—when students mistake my requests to lower their voices as an invitation to discuss our noise level policy. Basically, I do everything but hang their A+ papers on the staff lounge refrigerator.

I like being a mom. I'm pretty sure I didn't think I would when I was studying cataloging in library school, but I do. I enjoy parenting all of my kids, even the ones I didn't know I had until they wandered through my office door. When you sign up to become a mother, you don't necessarily get to choose the hours. It's a twenty-four hour, three hundred sixty-five days per year commitment. It's giving help when help is needed, caring when somebody needs you to care about what they're doing with their life. It's supporting a person's hopes and dreams. And, more often than not, it's giving a swift kick in the ass when necessary.

So that's what I do. No matter where I go, I'm a mom. I am a mom at work, and a mom at home. The crazy thing is, even though sometimes I might take it a bit too far, I think for the most part I've got it balanced pretty darn well. I mean, my daughters are rockin' hand-knitted rainbow scarves and my student worker knows when she sees a certain look on my face that she needs to back the fuck up and go make those copies I asked for a half hour ago.

I Still Just Want to Pee Alone

So, yeah.

JANEL MILLS *is the librarian/thug behind the blog* <u>649.133: Girls, the Care and Maintenance Of</u>, *where she writes about raising a princess, a wild child, and the sassiest redhead on Earth using as many curse words as possible. Janel is a contributor to Nick Mom, several wildly successful anthologies including* I Just Want to Be Alone, *and has also been featured on The Mighty, Scary Mommy, and The Huffington Post. When not blogging or librarian-ing, she keeps busy raising three beautiful little girls with her beardedly gifted husband in the wilds of metro Detroit.*

Potty Mouth
By Amanda Mushro
Questionable Choices in Parenting

When you become a mom, you get really good at dealing with other people's shit.

Literally.

Mere moments into this motherhood gig and you're already inundated by someone else's shit. No matter how many of your own kids you add into this shitty equation, you are a mom and you can totally handle it whether it's on their little bottoms, up their back, smeared on the wall, or attached to your pontytail. However, when it's fecal matter associated with someone other than a person you grew in your uterus, well that shit just ain't cool.

"Total rookie mistake," I muttered over the tears and whining of my children. I'd spent too long perusing the dollar bins at Target and both kids were melting down in unison. We were dangerously close to lunchtime, and after chugging the last few gulps of my Starbucks, I came up with two possible solutions: shove a bag of Goldfish crackers at them or abandon the cart full of randomness and get them actual food.

Through the automatic doors of Target, I had an Applebee's in sight. Even though Applebee's might not be in the fine dining category, I knew they wouldn't judge me when my kids dropped mac and cheese on the ground and better yet, they'd feed my unhappy campers quickly.

With perfect timing, nature called the exact moment our waiter set our food in front of us. "Mommy, I have to poop," chirped my boy. Since his poop-warning-window is approximately three minutes, I tucked a kid under each arm and dashed into the bathroom.

Now, I've never considered myself a germaphobe, but recently the only show that's on television during naptime is Dr. Oz, and the good doctor had an entire show dedicated to the lack of cleanliness in public bathrooms. The phrase "Millions of poop particles floating in the air" may have been repeated several hundred times in one episode. Since we've already established that I cannot handle the idea of someone else's poop particles, I sure as shit didn't want millions of those poop particles on me or my kids.

"Don't touch anything. Do you both hear me?" was the warning shot I fired off as I locked the door to the bathroom stall, but alas, it was too late. I spun around to find my boy climbing onto the toilet completely naked. He had somehow managed to disrobe before settling on the Applebee's throne. Socks, shoes, t-shirt, shorts, and Underoos were all scattered along the filthy bathroom floor. I couldn't even whip up a patchwork quilt made of thin toilet paper scraps just to cover the seat and give me a false sense of disease protection.

I scooped up his clothes and planned how I could properly disinfect his skin with something in my diaper bag. I was so preoccupied with avoiding poop particles, I nearly missed his newly toddling sister making a run for it by slithering under the stall door. I grabbed the escape artist by the ankle and dragged her back under the door.

"Millions of poop particles," I chanted over and over.

"Oh please stop touching things," I pleaded with the naked pooper. "Buddy, let's just keep your socks and shoes on because it's really, really yucky in here."

"Nope, can't do that Mommy. Wanna play I Spy?"

"Sure, I spy Batman underwear. Let's put them on!"

"Nope. I spy something blue."

No matter what we did, I couldn't keep my eyes off his chubby little hands. They were quick and everywhere: on the toilet seat, in his ears, on his manhood, rubbing his eyes, a quick scratch of his butt, and then his fingers were in his mouth.

Millions of poop particles.

Surely I was going to have to douse this kid in anti-bacterial soap upon completion of his "business." *Maybe I could power wash both kids at the gas station across the street?* I wondered.

After several rousing renditions of the ABCs and three hundred seventy-five rounds of I Spy, he announced he was done and my plan to run both kids through the restaurant dishwasher could now commence.

"OK, Buddy, let get you dressed and cleaned off." I was

relieved. We'd made it!

But as if in slow motion, I saw him stumble as he climbed off the potty. My motherly instinct was to reach out for him and break his fall. But that naked little man didn't need me to catch him because he was already reaching out to grab for something, anything.

He found his stability by using those tiny poop particle-covered fingers to grasp my face. He fish hooked me in the mouth with one hand while the other hand wrapped around my ear.

"Phew," he sighed. "I almost fell, Mommy!"

But I couldn't hear him because I knew that someone else's shit was in my mouth.

Millions of poop particles!

That was it. Just rename me Patient Zero.

In that moment, I imagined Ebola must be taking over my system, and I glanced over to see my daughter licking the toilet paper holder.

Well, at least we are all in this together, I thought through my delirium.

After the incubation time for symptoms of herpes, scabies, and all other airborne pathogens had passed, I realized we were in the clear from a potential disease ridden shit storm. However from now on, I will be fully prepared to watch the clock more carefully, always carry economy sized bottles of hand sanitizer, switch from Dr. Oz to Dr. Phil, and don't sweat the small shit.

AMANDA MUSHRO is the writer behind Questionable Choices in Parenting. Sometimes she thinks she's doing a great job as a mom, but then she does something that makes her question her own parenting abilities. She lives in Maryland with her family and once said being a stay-at-home mom meant she would have time to keep the house spotless and make homemade meals. This was the first of many times she would be completely wrong about parenting. Her writing has been featured on Scary Mommy and The Huffington Post. She is the director of Listen to Your Mother: Pittsburgh and has essays featured in five anthologies.

You Can Only Push a Mother So Far
By Alyson Herzig
The Shitastrophy

When I was pregnant with my first child I knew motherhood would test me, but I naively thought I could handle whatever came my way. I read all the books in preparation for my son's arrival, watched TLC's *A Baby Story* on continuum, and searched the Internet to absorb as much information as humanly possible. If knowledge was power then I was one step away from being Supermom.

Then I had my son Jacob and realized how asinine I had been.

Jacob could best be described as a spirited child—inquisitive and rambunctious. His curious little hands, when not clutching his beloved Superman figurine, were into everything. He wandered away whenever anything caught his eye. I always said if he were kidnapped they would return him after they realized how high maintenance he was. My other saying for Jacob is he should thank God he is so damn cute because it has saved his ass more times than I can count.

Jacob wasn't an easy child. When he was twelve months old we cut a vacation short when he decided to pledge a fraternity by throwing his crap all over the hotel room, vomiting from hysterical crying, running out in the parking lot naked, and staying awake for seventy-two hours straight. On the trip home I spent eight hours walking in circles in the airport because soon as the stroller stopped he screamed like a schoolgirl at her first Taylor Swift concert. It was as near to a death march as I have ever been.

Jacob kept me constantly on my toes. Either he was swimming in Tide laundry detergent (you have no idea how much that shit bubbles) or he was hell bent on escaping the confines of our home. If I foolishly tried to go to the bathroom alone I would hear the kitchen chair sliding over the tile floor to the patio door in order to unlock it. I can't tell you how many times I came out of the bathroom with my pants unbuttoned just in time to witness him break for the woods that abut our property.

Because I am a horrible planner, our daughter Jillian was born when Jacob was entering his terrible twos. This proved to be challenging in the same way, say, scaling Mt. Everest naked might be. I had no family nearby, sporadic babysitters at best, and a husband who traveled almost constantly. I was forever alone with both kids for long stretches of time, unless you count the checkout clerks at Target. What I needed was a pinch-hitter every so often, but one never came.

Some parents love this one-on-one time with their children. They relish the idea that their kids are only young once and this time cannot be made up. Everyone gets along and they probably make cookies and baby food from fucking scratch. My reality was very different. I was eternally exhausted and frustrated. I was covered in food stains and reeked of vomit. Showering was optional and sleeping more than a few hours at a clip was a fantasy.

I had very little patience during those toddler years, much like now, and thrived on adult interaction to break up the daily monotony of motherhood. Our recreational circuit involved the usual spots: various parks, the zoo, and local library. Sometimes we simply went to the mall and sat in the play space. I desperately needed other women to commiserate with; to tell me I was not alone in what I perceived to be the insanity of being a stay-at-home mother.

One place we went often was the inflatable bouncers. I looked past the Petri dish of bodily fluids and chose to focus on how much energy they burned. I got the most return on my bounce-house time investment, until it was time to leave. Jacob would pitch such a fit leaving that most times I carried him out tucked under my arm like a prized handbag, or over my shoulder like a bag of dog food. It was one of those berserk, bounce-house breakdowns when I finally lost my mind. I cracked like a fucking eggshell.

I informed Jacob we would be leaving in a few minutes; advance notice was always required to head off any potential tantrum. I then became distracted by Jillian and lost sight of him. When it was time to go, I realized he was missing. I became frantic with worry, and then I spied him, behind the fucking fence next to the large industrial fans.

After luring him away from the swirling blades of death I

dragged him over to the bench to put on his sneakers. I was sweating and shaking with anger and fear—a horrible combination—at his disobedience. I hoisted his hysterical, flailing body over my shoulder and carried him to the car like so many times before. Jillian recognized my despair and happily complied, while Jake refused to even sit in his booster seat. He assumed the rigid pose all parents know and hate.

After two years of dealing with Jacob's temper tantrums I had realized, with the help of a family therapist at over a hundred dollars per hour, that the more irate and agitated *I* became, the more *his* fits would escalate. I would need to be calm and patient in order to diffuse the situation. What I wanted to do was yank his disrespectful ass out of the car and string him up in the nearest tree by his pants with a sign advertising "Free Child." Instead I fixed an eerie Joker-like smile on my face and didn't say a word. This is not the easiest feat for even the calmest and kindest of mothers. Since I am neither of those things I might have had better luck sailing around the world in a rowboat with one arm.

Eventually I strapped my wooden child into his car seat and proceeded to get back into the car. I was livid and doing everything to calm my breathing in hopes of not engulfing in flames. As I reversed the car, Jacob looked at me, smiled, and unbuckled his seat belt.

Son of a bitch.

I threw the car in park, and exited the vehicle. How this kid didn't realize how close to death he was I had no idea. I flung open his car door and he scrambled over the seats to the back of the minivan. I climbed into the van, panting with fury, and dragged him to his seat. I re-buckled him without a word. I continued to focus on my breathing; I'd finally found a purpose for those stupid Lamaze classes. I didn't display even an ounce of anger, but you can bet your ass I was seething. If there was a chance of winning an Oscar for this performance I was sure to be a front-runner.

I regrouped, coolly entered the car, and began to reverse when Jacob sealed his fate. He looked at me, smiled, and unbuckled his seat belt.

MOTHERFUCKER!

Blind rage took hold of my body and I did the most horrible, despicable mother-move ever. My eyes locked on his coveted Superman grasped in his little dirty hand. Without thinking I grabbed The Man of Steel right from his clutches, and in one swift move, hurled Superman out the window! At that moment it was either Superman or Jacob. In retrospect, tossing Jacob to the curb for a five minute time-out may have been the more mature move.

As I proceeded to exit the parking lot Jacob became unhinged screaming, "No! Superman!" I looked at him in the rear view mirror. He was sobbing for his beloved figure and knew. I gripped the steering wheel fighting back the tears of frustration. I glanced at my daughter who sat silently in her car seat. I put my head on the wheel in defeat; I had allowed my emotions to get the best of me.

I looked at Jacob and spit out the words, "Sit in your seat and put your seat belt on *now!*" I was shocked when he complied. He must have finally understood he had pushed me too far. I circled the parking lot while he sobbed with his little four-year-old hand outstretched for his beloved Superman; tears streaming down his face at the horror that Big Blue had been sent airborne by his own mother. I parked the car and rescued Superman from the hard concrete; I'm not a total asshole.

I realize I shouldn't have thrown his toy out of the car window, but I would be lying if I said it didn't feel good for the few seconds I watched Superman soar through the air. The Man of Steel may not have saved my son that day, but he did rescue me from a dark moment.

A few months after Clark Kent's alter ego took off on his epic flight I had another horrible mom moment. It, too, was based on poor judgment, but more haphazardly than intentional. It had been yet another particularly stressful day with my little button-pusher Jacob and I had reached the breaking point. Where was my pinch-hitter, the television, to give me a break while I rocked in a corner? In another attempt to find solace and adult camaraderie, we visited a newly opened restaurant with an indoor playground. Upon leaving, each child selected a balloon, one of their favorite things, before heading to the car. Balloons for my kids were like crack, they couldn't get enough of them and I lived in fear of them popping. Our dining room had become a graveyard of deflated balloons rolling around on the carpet, but I didn't dare toss them—the fallout wasn't worth it.

While I was leaning into the car to buckle Jacob's seat belt he repeatedly hit me in the head with his balloon. No good deed ever went unpunished with this kid. When I pulled out of the parking lot Jacob continued to hit both his sister and I with the balloon. I repeatedly asked him to stop, but he wouldn't. *Breathe in and out.* He just smiled and chuckled after each bop. It was all a big game for him, but not for long.

I was overdressed and hot with anger when I unwittingly opened up the sunroof to get some fresh air and clear my mind. Before I knew it, the blue balloon was ripped out of Jacob's little hand and sent skyward. Jacob screamed and again reached his hand outward towards the sky, in an all too familiar scene, but this time there was no retrieving his coveted item. Instead I looked up and watched the balloon sail to the stratosphere, and smirked inwardly. Again I felt the sweet release of the day's stress and anger.

Jacob never did unbuckle his seat belt after Superman's flight and he never bopped me in the head again with another balloon. I later told our family therapist what I had done; call it mother's guilt that cost another hundred and twenty-five bucks. My therapist and I have crossed paths many times since then, in fact, our children go to the same school now, and he has confided in me that in all of his years of counseling "Superman's Flight" is one of his favorite stories. So I guess I'm not that bad of a mother. Either that or I need a new therapist.

Originally from New Jersey, ALYSON HERZIG lives in the Midwest but has kept her sarcastic cynical Jersey attitude. She has been described as the Andy Rooney of Stay-at-Home Moms. You can find her blogging about the perpetual shit storm of her life and various ridiculous observations at The Shitastrophy. *She is the co-creator of the anthology* Surviving Mental Illness Through Humor *released in April 2015, be sure to follow along this ground breaking mental health series at* SurviveMentalIllness.com. *She has also had works featured at Scary Mommy, The Huffington Post, Mamapedia, and other online venues.*

May you always poop alone!

Alyson
The Shitastrophy

Why, Mommy? And the Perfect Gift
by Kris Amels
Why, Mommy?

A few years ago, some asshole said, "Forty is the new twenty." I'll admit that I'm not very good at math, but I still call bullshit.

I'm forty-six and I have a three-year-old. Child-raising sometimes makes me wish I were twenty, and still enjoying that bottomless energy I had back then. However, I am not, and so I am mired in exhaustion so unbelievable it seems like Ripley could sell tickets to it. I think forty is more like the new sixty. What I do have now, at my ripe old age, is patience. I figure it's nearly as good as energy. And what I want, what I really, really want, is a night to myself. Just one. In a hotel. With twelve hundred thread count sheets. ALONE.

As I said, I have a three-year-old daughter. Yes, she was a complete (and completely welcome) surprise. No, I was not ready for the vigorously enforced intimacy that comes with having children. Her name is Isobel and she's my necklace; it doesn't matter what I'm doing, she's attached to me somehow. Forget peeing alone; she tries to help me wipe my ass. She's funny and helpful and sweet and adorable and all of these things only stop when she's sleeping ... and then I listen to her breathing on the monitor. I was not ready for this momdar that never turns off. Who knew? Well, you Moms knew, but nobody told me. You also knew we never, ever get a day off from mom-ing.

Have I mentioned that my kid is helpful? She's forcefully helpful. Fortunately, she's also super sweet. But, seriously, sometimes I'd like to have a few hours to myself. I just never get a break. For instance, the other morning while I was getting dressed, Isobel noticed a little hole in my underpants.

"Mommy, why is there a hole in your underpants?"

"They're old, Is. But it's okay, they're clean ... and nobody knows but us, right?"

She agreed with me. "Yep!"

A few hours later, Grandma came over, and Is had a lot to report.

"Grandma! Mommy has a hole in her underpants!"

Why, Mommy?

"Uh ..." My mother-in-law looked at me. I think she was horrified.

Is helped out here. "But it's okay, Grandma. Only we know. And they're clean."

I remember when we were at Grandma's for Easter dinner last year, the house full of relatives. I was sitting on the porch, chatting with some cousins when Is ran up to me and patted my belly so gently. Then she asked, "Mommy, why do you have a big belly?"

Mortified, I said, "I don't know, Is, I guess it goes with my big boobs and my big butt."

"Okay, then!" She hugged me, blew me a kiss, and ran back into the dining room while our audience of cousins laughed and laughed. Good times.

Shortly after that, because my memory is totally shot, I started a Facebook page called, Why, Mommy? to keep track of all the crazy things she asks me. All day, every day. I figure someday I'll look back on it and laugh, you know, maybe when she's in HIGH SCHOOL and I'm in my SIXTIES. You know, ha fuckin' ha. Where's my Geritol?

I don't know if you can relate. I previously had nothing BUT time to myself and then, suddenly I had exactly ZERO time to myself. My husband and I were together for twenty years before I got pregnant. We traveled a lot. Enough to have favorite places in a dozen cities. We had a mid-century modern home we took pride in restoring. Now it's full of Legos, crayons and flamingos, and no, we still haven't restored the basement wet bar. It's on the list. We promise. And no matter how much I love being a mom, sometimes, I really miss being alone.

It took me twenty minutes yesterday to write a five sentence email because I had to stop and play Tic Tac Toe with Is approximately four hundred times. I also had to let her win. She's only three, after all.

Whenever my husband asks me what I'd like as a gift—for my birthday, Christmas, Mother's Day, I tell him I'd like a night in a hotel with room service. Not a romantic night with him, no. Not that

that wouldn't be lovely. No. I really just want to be alone. Some days, I really, REALLY want to be alone. Just for a little while. I'll come back, I promise. I love my family, but I'm too old for this shit and I need a fucking break.

The other day, I was getting dressed, again with my adoring audience. Isobel watched me, hawk like. The kid misses nothing. She asked me, "Mommy, why are you wearing that leopard print bra?"

"I don't know, Is, it was the one on top in the drawer."

"But why aren't you wearing the BLAAAAACK bra?"

"It's in the wash."

"Oh. Why don't flamingos wear bras?"

"Because they don't have boobs."

"Oh! Okay."

Right after having this discussion, I had a little fantasy in my head where I would check into that magical gifted hotel room, drop my bag on the chair, and flop onto the nicely made bed with super fluffy pillows, falling asleep instantly.

And I would sleep. I would sleep and sleep and sleep and... wait.

I just had this conversation with Isobel a week ago, when she woke me up at six-thirty in the morning by running into my room and jumping on my bed, carrying two of her favorite flamingos. She had the biggest smile on her little face, and her eyeglasses were a bit crooked on her nose.

"Good morning, Is! Did you sleep well?"

"Mommy, I was sleepin', and sleepin', and sleepin', and sleepin', and sleepin', and sleepin', and sleepin', and sleepin' and then I woke up!"

"Wow!"

"Did you do dat, Mommy?"

"Yes. I was sleeping and sleeping and then I woke up."

"Only two sleeps?"

"Well, I had some laundry to finish after you went to bed, so yeah, I had a little less sleep than you."

The smile left her face. "Oh. That's too bad."

That is too bad, indeed. I would really, really like more than two sleeps. And I would like them in that hotel bed that someone else made. And I would like them ALONE.

And then when I wake up, I will use the bathroom. ALONE. I will get to poo in peace. Lately, my wildly helpful child has taken to coming into the bathroom and hugging me while I am on the toilet. It's sweet, yes. But damn! And it's getting worse.   About two weeks ago, she decided I needed help pooping. I was minding (and doing) my own business, when Is came racing into the bathroom and threw her arms around me.

"Mommy, are you pooping?"

"Yes. How about you go back to playing with your Legos? I'll be done in a minute."

"NO! I'm gonna help you push the poop out!" And she stood back, placed her hands against my abdomen, and pushed—hard. She's unreasonably big and Bam-Bam strong for a three-year-old; she nearly knocked me off the throne.

"Uh, hey, thanks. I can take it from here."

"You're welcome!" she chirped brightly and wandered off.

You see? How can I even get upset with her? She's ADORABLE.

But like I said, I could really use a break. Just this morning, I stepped out of the tub, and Is was hanging out on the pink yoga mat I put on the floor for her to play on while I'm showering. She looked up at me, so cute, curly hair messy from sleep, eyeglasses askew no matter how many times I take her to the eyeglass place and the guy straightens them, and she said, "Mom! Your boobs are HILARIOUS!"

As if that wasn't enough, the next thing she did was point the iPhone she had been playing with at me while I was drying off, and snapped a NSFW photo.

"Mom! I took a picture of your boob!"

"Uh ... "

"Oh ho! Two more pictures!"

"Is, please stop taking pictures of my boob."

"No way, Mom!"

I tried to escape, but she followed me into the bedroom to get dressed. She then wandered back to my bathroom, sat on the floor, pointed the phone at the toilet, and said, "Mom! I took a picture of the toilet!"

"Oh ... "

"Yes! Lots more pictures of the toilet!"

And I got that image of the hotel room in my head one more time. The made bed. The empty bathroom. Room service. A mini bar full of teeny-tiny icy cold vodka bottles, all just waiting for me. I let it wash over me like a visual mantra. And I closed my eyes for a moment and imagined.

For my gift hotel evening, Room Service will bring me a meal which I do not have to plan, buy, cook, clean up after, and then have contribute to the dishes of Sisyphus situation in my kitchen.

And don't forget what's waiting in the mini bar! I will take one little bottle of vodka. And I will not have to explain (again) to my daughter why she may not have a taste of Mommy's vodka. Because we've been over that several times already. And then I will eat my Room Service meal. While it is hot. ALONE.

About a week ago, Is was hanging out with me in the kitchen while I made dinner, as always. As I was cutting up carrots to roast, I ate a piece, and Is asked to try some. So I cut a few little pieces and put them on a napkin in front of her. She ate some and said, "Mom! I like carrots!"

"Great! These are raw, and I'm roasting these other ones with butter and thyme. I bet you'll like them, too."

She ate a few more pieces and then started spitting them out. Isobel took the napkin and rubbed her tongue with it.

"Is, what's wrong?"

"I don't like carrots!"

I couldn't believe it. "But you liked them a minute ago!"

"Mom! I keep tryin' all these foods I don't like!"

I'm just looking for one small break, here. I don't know if they'll really give me that night off in a hotel. Probably not. But I'm going to keep hoping, and keep that little picture in my head of dropping my overnight bag and flopping onto that big bed. ALONE.

Why, Mommy?

And I just overheard this: I wandered away from Is while she was using the toilet, so her dad went in to hang out with her for a few minutes while she finished making poo.

"Hey, Dad! Take a video!"

"Uh ... no."

Maybe we should make plans for a romantic night together in that magical hotel, after all.

KRIS AMELS is a fabulously frazzled frau, ex-reform-school-kid, and crazy art mom. At forty-six, she's still sorta surprised to have a three-year-old daughter (although she's become a big fan of hugs from said kid). Both mom and daughter have hip dysplasia, but it's cool; they can rock the body cast look. Kris landed a great husband, who's fortunately strong enough to carry around a forty-pound kid in a Spica cast. She thinks the world needs more pink glitter on it. And gold. And rhinestones. You can find her on Facebook or her blog, Why, Mommy?, when she has ten minutes to herself.

For Whom the Cow Moos
By Bethany Thies
Bad Parenting Moments

"I wonder if my mother-in-law likes my tits."

That's what I was thinking as she and I sat across from each other in my living room. We sat breast to face, me and the woman who birthed my husband and his twelve siblings, engaged in the world's most awkward staring contest.

We did not know each other well and perhaps I should have considered going into the bedroom to pump, but, I was the kind of tired you can only be after your first few nights home with a newborn. The kind of tired that helps you make the decision to completely disrobe in front of your in-law. The kind of tired that doesn't seem to bat an eye as you attempt to make conversation with a near stranger while your nipples are vacuumed into plastic cones.

The sound of the pump was the only sound in the room and then it happened. I looked up, stared directly into my mother-in-law's eyes and said, "Moo, moo. Moo, moo," in unison with the whir of the pump.

She looked at me with a mixture of amusement and confusion and so I did what any rational person would do. I did it again. "Moo, moo. Moo, moo."

This time I tried to make it sound a bit more mechanical, you know, to really drive the point home that I was a certifiable lunatic.

And then, God himself could no longer bear to watch my Fisher Price See 'n Say mental breakdown for one moment longer and sent my husband into the kitchen.

"What are you doing?"

"I'm a mechanical cow. I'm making mechanical cow noises."

"Ooooooooooh-kay. Did you get any sleep last night?"

"Yes. I had this wonderful dream that a woman in a white nightgown nursed our child for the entire night."

"Honey, that was you. You were wearing a white nightgown. You nursed our daughter all night."

"I don't think so. It was a dream. Besides, that lady looked like shit. All disheveled and with huge bags under her eyes and leaking milk and oh my God, it WAS me! Moo, moo. Moo, moo. Moo, moo."

"Honey … " He was afraid. The creepy twins standing outside of the elevator at the Overlook Hotel kind of afraid.

"Moo-ma-moo. Moo-a-moomoo. Moo, moo. Moo. Moo. Moo. Moo, mooooooo." I thought I'd switch it up a bit. No one likes a one-trick pony.

My mother-in-law had made the long trek from the east coast to meet her newest grandchild. We'd only met twice before. We'd been introduced the previous December when her son and I, only three weeks into our courtship, were grossly inebriated by new love. Our second meeting took place six months later at our Las Vegas wedding. I was three months pregnant. The daughter-in-law of her dreams. And now, here she was, trapped in a ratty duplex in Los Angeles with her son, newborn granddaughter, and a mooing daughter-in-law who refused to break eye contact.

"Moo. Moo, moo. Moo, moo, moo. Moo, moo. Moo."

At this point I had to own it. There was no going back. I was mooing for the rest of my life. I was Doc Brown and this pump was my time machine. Where we were going, we wouldn't need roads … or words.

The bottles of milk were now full and spurting over onto the dining room table; the pump making a guttural choking noise—its impassioned 911 call.

"Ma'am, we're here to help. Everything is going to be all right. Turn the pump to the off position and remove your breasts from the cones! Ma'am! Ma'am! I need you to focus. The valves are clogged! REMOVE YOUR CHESTICLES !"

I finally had my Aha! moment, stopped the pump and detached myself from the machine. I was wearing a hands-free pumping bra so the cones remained firmly attached to my chest. I stood up and milk began to drip-drip-drop from the plastic cones and puddle on the table. There I stood exposed for what I really was—the world's least sexy Fembot.

But while I stood in front of this woman I barely knew, I felt none of the things I should have been feeling: shame, embarrassment, my wet shirt. Nothing about this moment felt unnatural or worrisome and I remain thankful to the drug-like coma of new motherhood for this small gift.

And my beautiful mother-in-law, mother of thirteen children, took it all in without noticeably wincing because I was not just her son's wife anymore. I was a mother. We now belonged to the same club of women who loved a small creature enough to completely deconstruct ourselves. I stood in front of her, breasts exposed, just a mom trying to feed her baby. She watched me fall apart with not one ounce of judgment; just a mom who understood the out of body experience I was having. My breasts were no longer my breasts and the people in my living room may as well hear me moo and cry and struggle with diaper changes. They may as well enjoy the ride. And if they didn't? Well, I was willing to slow the carousel down to twenty-five miles per hour. They could tuck and roll while I wiped spit-up on the arm of my robe and carried on with my day.

Standing had shifted my shirt and left my stomach completely exposed. I suddenly became conscious of my swollen, soft midsection. She noticed me notice. "You look wonderful! I can't believe you just had a baby a few days ago." she exclaimed. I would have kissed her on the mouth, but I hadn't brushed my teeth in three days.

Just then, my daughter woke up. She was dressed for company with a tiny bow stuck to her mostly bald head. She looked like a sixty-year-old man dressed in drag. "Isn't she beautiful?" I asked, looking desperately for a way to start over. A way to say, "Heyyyy, sorry about those last twenty minutes of random mooing. We cool?"

She grabbed my hand and said, "Oh, she's absolutely perfect." And then I knew that my bare chested barnyard bevy of poor decision making didn't matter one bit.

We're all connected in the overwhelming love and insanity of the job. The only gift we have to offer each other is grace.

Bad Parenting Moments

BETHANY THIES is a writer and the (mostly) proud mother of four Vikings. She details her blunders, misadventures and the joyful chaos of parenting on her blog Bad Parenting Moments. She can often be found searching for her self-respect, lost youth, keys and discount non-perishables. Bethany will write for food and has original works published in several best-selling anthologies. She contributes regularly to her local, independent newspaper and can be heard on Vermont radio every week. Her children are unimpressed.

You can connect with Bethany on Facebook, Twitter, Google+ and other virtual spaces where people avoid religious debate and eye contact.

The Very Strict Code For Female Behavior
By Harmony Hobbs
Modern Mommy Madness

Before I met my husband, my love life was a series of unfortunate events.

Let's begin with second grade, when I had a crush on a boy named Sam. He was a year older and very tall—my heart fluttered when I landed the spot next to him at the school Christmas program. One day during practice, I lost my footing on the bleachers, and as my leg slipped through the gap I reached out, grabbing for anything. I grabbed his pants ... which came down with me.

He hated me from that point on.

In sixth grade, I had a boyfriend who I was too shy to talk to. "How is that possible," you ask? I don't really know, but it was painfully awkward. We were in the same class, but only communicated through notes. When it became apparent to him that I wasn't going to be putting out (since I wouldn't even walk next to him in the hall), he broke up with me—via note, of course—for an older woman. I'll spare you the traumatic details of the next ten years (you're welcome), but suffice it to say that by the time I met my husband I'd developed a very strict code for dating behavior which was built upon a variety of embarrassing experiences.

The Very Strict Code For Female Behavior:

1. Never let him see you without concealer. Never let him experience a hairy leg. Never create any evidence whatsoever that you poop. You're a *woman*, for God's sake.
2. You do not throw up anywhere but in the bathroom. Not in his car, not on the side of the road, and most definitely not on him. You can hold it in until you are in the safety of a lavatory. Swallow that shit and be a *lady*, dammit.
3. Always wait for him to call you. You do not call him. It's fine to obsess over him while you wait, that's what your girlfriends are for. Just do not call. Keep that psycho bitch side hidden away for as long as possible. Preferably until after the honeymoon.

4. Bras and panties should always match. You want to get laid, don't you?! But not until you've shown him that you aren't a whore.
5. Never, ever, pass gas in his presence. Women do not have gas.

I know, I know—this is the lamest crock of shit you've ever read. I agree, it really is a crock of shit. Don't give up on me just yet.

At the beginning of the relationship with my now-husband, I would tiptoe out of bed to apply just the right amount of concealer and mascara in an effort to look goddess-like when he first opened his eyes. I couldn't put *too* much on or it would be obvious that I'd tampered with myself. This is an art I spent a lot of time perfecting. I declined to shower with him, lest he see the awful truth of my face with makeup running down it.

He was the first man who I felt truly understood and accepted me, but I wasn't willing to share my so-called unattractive side with him. Unfortunately for me, I'm terrible at hiding my unattractive side. I'm clumsy. I drink too much. I don't have good night vision, and my day vision isn't much better. If it weren't for the miracle of optometry, I would be bumping around on the streets with a cane right now.

Over time, one by one, the rules of The Very Strict Code For Female Behavior eroded. That man had to take care of me, hold back my hair, and bring me wet washcloths when I was sick. One time I got food poisoning and threw up so hard that I hit the bridge of my nose on the sink faucet, which resulted in me lounging around sans makeup with under eye bruising the next day. My husband was unfazed.

After we were married and made the ridiculous decision to become parents, he witnessed three vaginal births ... starting with the time that we stupidly agreed that he should be my "birthing partner." We both assumed that meant he would be standing supportively by my head, holding my hand and whispering words of encouragement.

Nope.

I Still Just Want to Pee Alone

"Birthing partner" meant that he would be holding my right leg for me as I pushed for two hours to get a baby who was stuck on my tailbone out of my body, but he hung in there like a champ. Probably because he knew I'd choke him with my bare hands if he wimped out. He was the one who had to help me in and out out of bed in the hospital as unmentionable body fluids ran down my legs. He went to the store for mega-sized maxi pads, and shopped for a multitude of stool softeners and suppositories.

I tried to maintain my dignity throughout these situations.

I failed.

My bra and panty collection became the antithesis of sexy. My psychotic bitch side emerged—there was obviously no keeping that under wraps. My husband has seen me at my most beautiful and most atrocious and loves me anyway, yet the one self-imposed rule I continued to hold onto was rule number five: Women do *not* have gas.

Holding in my gasses, especially through pregnancy, was no easy feat, and left me with little sympathy for a man who says "I just couldn't hold it in." Oh really? You *couldn't*? Because when I had a small human jammed inside of my body, I somehow managed to hoist myself off the couch and walk to another room to spare you the experience of smelling a pregnant lady hummus-and-choco-late-chips-for-breakfast fart. You, sir, are just lazy and smelly.

I hung onto that tiny shred of dignity with everything that I had as if it was all I had left of my self-respect—because it was. It was all I had left of The Very Strict Code. But then, one night during a phone call with a friend, I downed a few glasses too many of wine and before I knew it the clock struck midnight and I was drunk.

Then, after almost twelve years together, I broke the last and final rule.

I let my first toot slip in front of him.

I was mortified.

I kept talking as if nothing happened, attempting to ignore the man in the same room who was laughing so hard that tears were olling down his face. Maybe he was crying from relief. Maybe he was crying tears of joy. Maybe he was devastated that his wife had finally broken the last rule in The Very Strict Code.

I stalked to the bathroom to carry out my bedtime routine, and as I fumbled with my contact lens case he finally choked out that our relationship had reached a whole new level. To my amazement, he interpreted this unfortunate event as the ultimate sign that I have accepted him completely after all this time.

In fact, he wanted to have sex.

Men are gross.

HARMONY HOBBS is a full-time mother of three who navigates the waters of motherhood without any grace or finesse whatsoever. She began her blog <u>Modern Mommy Madness</u> *as a way to cope, and has continued to self-medicate by writing all the things that she can't say out loud. A fan of strong coffee, red wine, and very sturdy undergarments, Harmony can be found on Twitter, Facebook, and in your local liquor store.*

Get the Fuck Out of My Shower
by Kathryn Leehane
Foxy Wine Pocket

I am a shower tyrant. I always have been. Much to my family's dismay, I don't want anyone with, near, or even in the vicinity of me when I'm showering.

I trace this back to my childhood. When I was in preschool, I would shower with my older sister. She would help me shampoo my hair and make sure I was cleaning all of my parts. The problem was that she stood in front of the shower nozzle the entire time, and would periodically lean from side to side to give me some of the spray. So most of the time, I was cold and yearning for an uninterrupted flow of warm water. Even at that tender age, I remember thinking, "Fuck this shit. I want my own damn shower."

Ever since then, I've always prized my solo shower time. It's my special time to think and relax and wash away the day prior. It is my Me Time.

My husband is not so thrilled with my shower stance, and it's been a difficult rule to enforce. I guess this is my fault, really. Early in our fornicating years, I may have indulged him with a little sexy time in the shower. But eventually that got old, and I put an end to it and reclaimed the stall as my own.

My God, now that I've said it out loud, that's as bad as a blow job bait-and-bail, isn't it?

For many years, I repeatedly rebuffed my husband's requests for a shared shower. "I'm trying to get clean! I don't need your goo on me!" I exclaimed more than once.

He then suggested we try showering together for intimacy, not sex. Every once in a while, I'd give in, but we discovered that we have different preferences for water temperature. He likes just barely warm water whereas I prefer water so hot that it practically melts off your face.

"Just get out," I insisted during one such lukewarm shower-for-two. There could be no temperature compromise. I reinforced the solo shower rule.

Once I had kids, however, solo shower time became an entirely different challenge. Even finding the time to hose off was difficult, let alone time to really enjoy myself. I'd squeeze it in during naptime or wake up at ungodly hours to ensure uninterrupted relaxation and cleansing.

I explained my dilemma to a friend, and she replied, "Why don't you just let your daughter play outside the stall while you're in there?"

I eyed her doubtfully. That didn't sound relaxing at all. She assured me it was possible. She suggested I bring a few toys and let my daughter play while I shower in peace.

I was right to be skeptical—it *wasn't* that easy. And it certainly wasn't peaceful. My child quickly bored of her own playthings and would search the room for other toys. She would make telescopes out of tampons (clean ones), stick maxi pad art on the wall (again, clean ones), and wreak general havoc in my bathroom. I tried to distract her by drawing pictures on the fogged up shower doors. That seemed to work for a while. I could shower mostly uninterrupted and only needed to pause occasionally to draw something for her to admire. It wasn't total relaxation, but it would have to do.

Then one day during shower time, she pointed to my stomach and said, "Baby."

I patted my fleshy pooch and looked down. "Great. Now my kid is insulting my baby weight too?! I thought that was just ~~my mother~~ me," I muttered to myself.

"No, sweetie, there's no baby in here."

She pointed more dramatically and raised her voice, "BABY!"

"No. There is NO baby in here. Mommy's tummy is just *really* big, all right?!"

"NO," she hollered and then crawled over to touch the shower door. "BABY!"

Oh.

My daughter didn't think I was pregnant. She just wanted me to draw a baby on the shower door.

Insecure much?

So then my solo shower time became about more than just attaining Zen. It was also about preserving my dignity. After that incident I made sure to get up early enough to shower without an audience or self-inflicted insult. Some days I would just skip it altogether. Cleanliness is overrated, right?

I managed a few years of interruption-free showers, and I was just getting my shower mojo back when my son ruined it for me. It started off innocent enough. He'd barge in during shower time and make some observations.

"Mommy, how come you don't have hairy boobies like Daddy?"

"Mommy, why is your tummy so mushy?"

"Mommy, how come you don't have hair on your 'gina anymore? You had some yesterday."

After that last one, I asked my son to please ~~get the fuck out~~ give me privacy in the bathroom. To please respect the closed door. That worked for a while, but the temptation was just too great, I suppose. Because he came in to ask me how many friends he could invite to his birthday party ... which was three months away. I sighed and answered his question as I dried off with a towel.

He examined my stomach through the shower stall and "helpfully" suggested, "You know, Mommy, you should really try Celtrixa. You could see dramatic results in two weeks."

"Uhhh, what now?"

"You know, those stretch marks on your stomach? You've got a lot of them, but Celtrixa reduces stretch marks by seventy-five percent. And it works on new *and* old stretch marks."

"I see. You know, just because the television tells you something, that doesn't always mean it's true. Can you please leave while I finish in here? Gimme a little privacy?"

"Uhhh, Mommy. Celtrixa has *clinically* proven results. And you can see dramatic results within two weeks. Two weeks!"

"Okay. Thanks for the information. Did you come in here for something specific?"

"I don't remember. But you should really consider Celtrixa."

"Okay then. It's time to leave the bathroom. Please get out. NOW."

After that final blow, I took more drastic measures to ensure my privacy. If that kid could recite commercials and clinical results, he could read and follow some explicit rules. I hung a sign outside my bathroom door that read:

**Unless someone is bleeding or the house is on fire,
DO NOT come in here when the door is closed.
Any violation will result in an automatic $20 fine."**

That did the trick, and I have my shower back from my children. Now if I could only keep my husband out. Because I'm quite certain he'd happily pay the twenty bucks.

KATHRYN LEEHANE is a writer and humorist living in the San Francisco Bay Area with her husband and two children. Along with inhaling books, bacon, and Pinot Noir, she writes the humor blog, Foxy Wine Pocket, where she shares twisted stories about her life as a mother, wife, friend, and wine-drinker in suburbia. She is a contributing author to several anthologies and is at work on her first manuscript. Her essays have also been featured on BLUNTmoms, The Huffington Post, Scary Mommy, In the Powder Room, and more. Follow Foxy Wine Pocket on Facebook and Twitter.

On Jesus and Ex-Lax
By Lola Lolita
Sammiches and Psych Meds

Of all the lady-like things I discuss with my husband and friends, pants crapping is at the top of the list. Most women have never had to deal with this phenomenon aside from that which has to do with their own children.

I am not most women.

I'm a delicate flower, one might say. A dainty feather of femininity. If Leonardo DaVinci set out to create yet another Mona Lisa, it would be my exquisite visage and shapely contours adorning his masterpiece, enticing art critics and lonely bachelors with my tender mystique. Just kidding. I'm the thorns on a rosebush or the nasty white thingies that fly off dandelions and populate perfectly manicured lawns with my devil spawn. If anyone set out to paint something with me as the subject, it would likely incorporate Dali-esque surrealism and anal suppositories. I don't whisper in my panties; I shart in those biotches. And I'm not afraid to talk about it.

Upon entering motherhood, most women have heard the horror stories about babies having up-the-back diaper drama and toddlers poo painting on the walls next to their cribs while their parents slumber unknowingly in the next room. Most women also don't expect the diarrhea up the back to be so bad that they consider throwing the baby out with the bath water and starting over with a new one, so to speak, or having to completely re-drywall because little Monet's poosterpiece is so existential, no amount of Magic Eraser will scrub those walls clean. This must have been how my husband felt upon entering marriage. Sure, he'd heard from his already married friends that, contrary to wishful thinking, the ladies in their lives actually *do* shit once in a while. But I'm certain he never expected the crapcapades involving his lover to be worse than those involving his offspring or for his offspring to have inherited the worst of Mommy's ass ailments, many of which are so bad, the daycare workers document them on the take-home activity charts with the simple yet menacing words, "BLOWOUT, THREE P.M." And in all honesty, even I never expected my family's tendency toward mud butt would be so extreme that tales of our toilet habits would become legendary in the childcare circle.

To be fair, I never chose to be so fucking disgusting. It chose me. I blame my irritable bowels and penchant for chili cheese fries. That and, in my earlier days, my addiction to cheap beer, hipstery cigarettes, and black coffee. You haven't experienced the horror that is a fiery o-ring until you've pulled an all-nighter with a case of Natty Light, a pack of Parliaments, and some gas station java festooned to your man hands. Which is why, try as I might to thwart my propensity for unexpected colon blasts in public situations by steering clear of any cuisine that might offend my surly innards, I am still rarely successful, so I have decided to embrace my explosive viscera. Violent tendencies toward bubble butt are not without their merits, believe it or not.

The first time I used my digestive bitchery for my own benefit was in college. My roommate and I were en route from the airport to our condemnable rental house after spending spring break in Denver, Colorado with a recently-graduated friend. I don't know if it was six straight nights of playing pool and bumming cigarettes from the fifty-something regulars at the Old Shillelagh (which I insisted on pronouncing as *shi / lay / laGCKGCKGCK* despite knowing full well how to actually say it) or not drinking enough water at such a high altitude that sent my tummy a-turning, but either way, about halfway to our destination I had to demand she pull over immediately so I could empty my last three-and-a-half meals on the expressway shoulder whilst clenching my ass cheeks like a Vise Grip on a woodworking bench to keep from defecating myself. To make matters worse, even after christening my toilet with a gallon of chickenshits and three-quarters of my spleen, I *still* couldn't get any relief from volcanic mud butt. Off to the hospital it was.

If you've ever wondered where society's least desirables go to congregate, it's the emergency room waiting area. The place smells of body odor and broken dreams and houses but a single perpetually occupied one-holer for the community's most rancid and toothless to dispense of their waste. On no fewer than three occasions during my hours-long wait did I have to sprint outside to avoid upchucking my pancreas on my neighboring ne'er-do-wells and painting the walls with my excrement before putting my foot down and pledging to do something—fucking *anything*—to speed this thing along.

"I have been here for two-and-a-half hours," I grumbled to the nurse perching comfortably behind a sliding glass window. "I can't wait anymore. Seriously. It smells like Satan's asshole out here."

"I'm sorry, ma'am." She continued examining her computer screen. "You're just going to have to be patient."

"I have been patient. I'm done being patient," I declared.

She stopped typing and peered at me. "Well, there's nothing I can do. Sorry."

"Really? Nothing you can do? How about I shit all over your waiting area? Is there something you can do then? Because I will. So help me God, I will shit my pants right here and now. I'm not kidding. I'm so not fucking kidding right now. It's coming. I can't hold it in. I will do it."

"She will," my roommate chimed. "She will definitely do it."

"Excuse me?" the nurse asked.

"I WILL SHIT ALL OVER THIS PLACE," I screamed, desperation pouring down my face in sweat droplets. Turns out, there was something she could do. I was on a hospital bed and hooked to an IV in under five.

I'd like to say this was my plan all along, this promising to release my penetralia upon the masses to get what I wanted STAT, but it wasn't until I was safely home in my bed, rehydrated and pumped full of meds, that I realized what an effective superpower I had been gifted. Gone were the days of feeling ashamed about my leaky hindquarters. I would no longer politely refuse jalapeno poppers and five alarm salsa at tailgates and holiday get-togethers, terrified of awaking the rumbling beast down under and having to wait for an open stall in a long line of gossipy sorority sisters with perfectly polished fingertips and daisies for rectums. I would indulge without abandon. I would gorge those motherfuckers gone and wait for the magic to happen, proudly proclaiming my impending expurgation and parting the seas like Moses whenever I felt the whim. I would-make the world my bitch, and my oozy taint would lead the charge.

I have used this malady with which I've been blessed to my advantage on numerous occasions: to jump the TSA security line, to use the twelve items or less checkout register at the grocery store when I have thirty items and three shrieking offspring in my cart, and to get the bank teller to let me in the building at closing time, to name a few. And each time I've employed this tactic to get my way, I've muttered a silent prayer that God never strip me of my fecal incontinence lest I be left to wait my turn for shit like the rest of the world's sorry saps.

Though I've attained great success in this endeavor, I feel compelled to caution my fellow intestinally challenged on the intricacies of executing this method should they decide to practice it in their own favor. Threatening to crap one's pants in an effort to get one's way isn't as easy as it would seem. The key lies in selling it and selling it hard. If you're not sweating like a hooker at Sunday mass and shaking all shifty-eyed like a tweeker going through withdrawals, you're not doing it right. Nobody will believe you're about to unleash Assagra Falls unless your face looks the appropriate amount of pained and your vocal cords vibrate at three octaves higher than normal. To really drive it home, I recommend squeezing off-key melodies out of your butt flute between begging Allah to have mercy on your entrails and vowing to murder the target's unborn children at maximum volume. Better yet? If your progeny have also been blessed with the gift of gross gut, employ them in your shenanigans. Hold family rehearsals between dinner and bedtime, coaching them in the art of looking forlorn and in blackmailing passersby with warnings to comply or else.

This is my gift to you. Sage advice from a seasoned shit burglar. Depending upon how Oscar-worthy your performance is, you can expect to abscond with anything from a warning instead of a speeding ticket to a meal on the house at your city's finest Italian establishment before anyone's the wiser. A word of warning, though: don't let your triumphs go to your head. Not even Jesus, what with turning water into wine and all, made it out of this world without drawing the scorn of jealous onlookers. And should you ever find yourself in the midst of a Judas, I recommend throwing back some Ex-Lax, washing it down with some Marlboro Reds and a hot pot of caffeinated sludge, and baptizing the offender's toilet good. They'll never entertain betraying your strategy again.

And that's a promise.

LOLA LOLITA is a mother, wife, educator, wine lover, and chronic sufferer from anxiety, immaturity, and children. When she's not busy scarring her kids for life, she can be found in her book, Who Pooped on the Corpses? And Other Pressing Life Concerns, on her blog, Sammiches and Psych Meds, and on Facebook and Twitter.

Afternoon Delight
By Rebecca Gallagher
Frugalista Blog

My husband and I are your poster people for vanilla sex. You know. Good ol' missionary style and really boring.

So one afternoon when we happened to be home alone, I headed up to the shower. I kinda hinted, Mae West style, "Wanna come up and see me sometime?" Hubs jumped at the chance. Because you know, married sex is also code for "once in a while sex."

I started the shower, running the water to get it hot before I got in. Can I be honest here? I really hoped that he'd give me a minute or two to so I could start exfoliating and deep conditioning.

Nope.

Bathroom door swings open and he's like an eager little boy getting in the car for the promise of a trip to the Lego Store. He strips off his underwear and tosses it on the floor. (Dear God, why not in the hamper? Why do they never get it in the hamper?) He jumps in the shower and joins me. And whaddya know, now I have no room under the warm water. Well I guess this means I have to get closer to hubs. Gosh dangit his hands are ice cold. Really? Okay, fine. Let's just get this going.

Me [reaching up to kiss him and producing a Niagara Falls shower off his nose and into my mouth since he's much taller and the shower head is directly behind him.]: Mmm, you're so … *(cough, sputter, cough, gag, choke)*

Him: Here, let me switch places with you. Yeah, baby that's it.

Me: Here, let me suds you up à la Christian Grey style.

Him: Who's Christian Grey?

Me: Never mind, I'll just wash you down like all sexy, m'kay?

Him: Yes, please!

Me: OH SOAP! There's soap in my *eye*! I think it's from my conditioner! I need to rinse. You wash your own back, I'm rinsing. We need one of those eye flushy things like in chemistry class. Oh my GOD, it burns! Ugh, wait a minute … O.K. … that's better.

Him: Let me get your back instead.

Me: Yeah, here's a loofah, I've got some bacne spots I can't reach back there. It'd be so great if you could scrub them for me.

Him: Hey, you have a mole here, are you going to get that checked out? Not to mention these rough sort of patches that look like …

Me: Barnacles? They look like barnacles, right? Yeah, my dermatologist has some fancy name but she calls them barnacles and told me they're common for fair skinned folks at my age.

Him: O.K. Let me wash your … barnacles …

Me: Oooh, your hands are warmer … So is the rest of you … Hey, want to get me right— (cough, choke, gag, sputter) Are you trying to drown me? Could you *move* so this doesn't keep happening?

Him: Sorry, there isn't much space for me. We need a two person shower one of these days.

Me: We need a whole new bathroom one of these days. These gold fixtures are the worst in tackiness and the grout is coming apart.

Him: Yeah, tell me about it. Maybe once we're done paying for soccer …

Me: And new shoes for the kids …

Him: We can have a new bathroom.

Me: Mmmm.

Some kissing and smoochy stuff ensues. Trying to be uber sexy while my eyes are still red and irritated from the previous soap mishap and trying not to slip on the shave foam residue is a little tricky.

Eventually I try to take things to the next level.

Me: Umm, maybe you should like, squat. You're too tall. Our whatsits don't match up when we stand.

Him: You could bend over.

Me: You could fly off a bridge. I am NOT bending over. What's that smell? Ew. Do you smell that? Oh yuck! It's this mildewy shampoo bottle. Look at the bottom of it. It's all black and it stinks.

Him: Could we focus on the reason we're in here. I mean, you look so great all wet and …

Me: What was that? Did you lock the front door? Did I just hear Owen back from his friend's house?

Him: Nah. It's probably neighbor kids outside. Keep doing that with your hand.

Me: No really, I think—

Owen [From the hall]: MOM, I'm home!

And scene.

You think shower sex looks good in the movies, huh? Well in the movies they have maids, fancy bath fixtures, and no small children under foot. Shower sex just isn't what it's cracked up to be.

REBECCA GALLAGHER is writer and creator of Frugalista Blog. She likes to share about her kids, husband, makeup and how to wear Spanx. She has been featured on The Huffington Post, Scary Mommy, Bonbon Break and TodayShow.com. She has entertained the masses at MamaCon in Seattle and even performed stand up comedy without people throwing fruit at her. Rebecca was also in the prequel, I Just Want to Pee Alone.

The Day I Got Taken to Church
By Ashley Allen
Big Top Family

You never forget your first time. I know I never will.

The first time my mom ever cursed in front of me, it was the summer of 1986, and I was twelve years old. If we're being technical, it wasn't a *verbal* curse word; she flipped me the bird. I don't remember *why* she did it, really, but I don't think that's integral to the story. What *is* integral to the story is that my mom was and is SUPER religious; like, the kind of religious person that God-talks your head off and makes you want to exorcise yourself. I'm all for God, but I once saw an Internet meme on this topic that sums up my feelings perfectly. It said "Religion is like a penis. It's fine if you have one, but once you start waving it in my face, we have a problem." My mom was a penis-waver. And when your super holy, angelic, penis-waver mom tells you to sit on it and spin with an obscene finger gesture, how do you think that affects a kid? I'll *tell* you how. That kid's WHOLE WORLD shatters into teeny, tiny, middle-finger-shaped shards.

I felt like the blinders had been removed from my naïve little eyes. If my mother, who I often likened to the Virgin Mary, was capable of sinking to the same level of depravity as my little pre-teen friends and I, then what other similar antics was she up to? Playing Spin the Bottle and Truth or Dare? Prank calling people she didn't like? Looking at confiscated *Playgirl* magazines? Experimenting with every single curse word known to man, sometimes stringing them along into one, long, compound cuss-word like my personal favorite, *shitfuckassdamn*?

It was a pivotal moment for me, and I started seeing the world in a different way. Adults weren't perfect; parents weren't infallible. The disturbing truth swirling around in my head was that they were probably a lot like us kids—they probably made mistakes all the time. And if they were capable of making mistakes, then I should be questioning, all the time, what I was being told by them. In essence, my mom didn't just give me the one finger salute that day; she kicked off a stage in my pre-adolescent life that should probably be entitled, "When I Became a Little Asshole."

Fast-forward to my life today as a mom of three boys (including a set of twins). I'm still an asshole, but I'm not so little anymore. When I started having kids, I told myself I wouldn't make the same mistakes my mom made. I would be myself—I would let them know from the get-go that Mama ain't no saint. But that, ahhh, umm, didn't really go as planned, you see, because you do have to give your kids models of socially appropriate behavior. You can't go around dropping "that's what she saids" willy-nilly in front of them, the way you do when you're drinking with your friends. You also can't tell a coffee table to go fuck itself when you stub your toe on it. I mean, you CAN, but just not in front of them. It's just not normal. Plus, they're so sweet and innocent and cute—why would you want to poison their little souls by letting them know their mom is basically the anti-Christ? That helps *nobody* sleep at night.

So. I amended my former plan, and at least when my kids were around, I metamorphosed into a "G-rated" version of myself. Unlike my mother, however, I was not going to top off my squeaky clean image with penis-waving. I did teach my kids the basics about God, took them to church on Easter and Christmas, and enrolled my oldest son, Sam, in a Christian pre-school, and I felt good about doing the absolute minimum. Everything was going fine and dandy. Until …

The great-grandparents started dropping like flies. Our twins, at two years old, were too young to know that their great-grandparents had died, but Sam took it much harder than I ever expected him to. He cried, he trembled, he asked what would happen to him if *we* died, what would happen to him if *he* died. To quell his fears, I started talking about Heaven and all of us meeting up again in the afterlife, and it seemed to put him at ease. He started asking to say prayers before bed, and of course we obliged. Next it was prayers before meals, like they did at school, so of course we obliged. Next it was—"Can we hang a cross in my room? Why don't we own any Bibles? Can you teach me the 'Our Father?' and Shouldn't we be going to church more?"—until I woke up one morning in a cold sweat and realized that Jimmy Freaking Swaggart was sleeping in a toddler bed down the hall.

I decided, though, that raising a little boy who cared about God and religion could actually be a *good* thing. It didn't mean he was going to turn into my penis-waving mom. It might simply mean that he would stand on a high moral ground and try to do and *say* good, nice things all the time. Sam would never have to know that, in actuality, after she clocked out of her day job, his mom had a mouth that would make Andrew Dice Clay sound like Joel Olsteen.

Everything was going fine and dandy until this little bastard on the bus—let's just call him "Dick"—taught Sam every single, last curse word known to sailors across the Seven Seas. Even how to spell them! Sam left home one day an innocent, ignorant second-grader and came home captain of his own salty swear ship. He flung down his backpack and began interrogating me about what all these new words meant, and I wasn't prepared. I just panted and told him they were very bad words and that he should never say them.

"But what do they *mean*, Mommy?" he persisted.

"Like, you want to know their definitions? Why?" I asked, beads of sweat soaking my pits.

"What if someone calls me one?" he answered. "I won't even know what I'm being called! I'll be stupid!"

I wasn't sure that was a valid argument, but shitfuckassdamn, what could it hurt now? He already knew the words. I sighed and defined one as a synonym for "bum," another as a synonym for "poop," and yet another as a synonym for "darn."

"Satisfied? Can we agree to never say these words now?" I pressed.

"You left one out. The one that starts with 'F.' You know, 'fewk,'" he whispered. I choked. I snorted. I swallowed. I cleared my throat.

"Oh. *That* word. Well, that's not how it's pronounced—it actually rhymes with 'duck.' But that is the worst word of them all, son. It has a lot of definitions and can be used just like 'darn,' but it's also the most insulting, awful thing you can say to someone. You just don't want to say it, O.K.?"

"O.K," he agreed solemnly. And all was once again fine and

dandy. Until ...

Until the night I was driving all three of the boys out of our neighborhood to go back-to-school shopping. I pulled our SUV onto a busy two-lane road. I was steadily gaining speed, but kept the car under the fifty-five mile-per-hour speed limit. I went up a slight hill and I noticed with a jolt that another SUV was coming straight towards me in my lane!

I carefully pumped the brakes, still not really sure what I was seeing, but the other car seemed to actually *accelerate*. I realized that I was not, in fact, hallucinating, and I started *really* slamming the brakes. Sippy cups and Nintendo DSs came flying at the dashboard and I instinctively screamed, "WHAT THE FUUUUUUUCK?!" And magically, the second the word "fuck" flew out of my mouth, the SOB pulled his SUV back into his lane behind the Mack truck he'd been trying to pass and whizzed safely past me.

My little twins had no clue what obscenity had just passed my lips. However, I caught sight of Sam's face in the rearview mirror, ashen and wide-eyed, like he'd just discovered his mother was not the Virgin Mary, but in fact, Lady Gaga.

"Sam," I began cautiously, like I was trapped with a caged tiger. "I-I-I'm sorry. I shouldn't have said that word. In my defense, I was really stressed out, and I actually thought we might die!"

"You thought we might *die*?" he asked, incredulous.

"Yes, or at least I thought we may get very, very hurt."

"You THOUGHT we might DIE?" he thundered.

"Umm," I was stuttering now. "Yes, sort of, at the time? Well, yes."

Still watching him in the rearview mirror, I saw Sam's expression transform suddenly from consternation to resignation. There was something vaguely familiar in it.

"You thought we might die." Sam shook his head slowly. "And *that* was the last word you thought we should hear, Mommy?"

ASHLEY ALLEN is a multi-task-dysfunctional mom of three boys, including a set of twins, and a survivor of a weird childhood. She writes a circusy, irreverent humor blog at <u>Big Top Family</u> *about her childhood and adulthood and always ends up finding that the bridge between them isn't as long as she thinks. Her stories have been published on The Huffington Post, Scary Mommy, and BluntMoms. When she's not blogging or juggling the family balls, she's posting her ridonkulous musings on Facebook and Twitter.*

When the Public Library Thwarted Me
By Meredith Spidel
The Mom of the Year

Before having children, I enjoyed a very symbiotic relationship with the public library. They had books they wanted to lend out, I wanted to read them. Using the wonders of the online reservation system, I put titles on hold in advance, later sneaking in at my convenience to take them home. It was glorious.

Then children entered the scene, along with their ungainly complex carseat buckles. I found myself begging my husband to scoop up books on his lunch break. I would drive to the next town over to return books as this library had a drive-thru drop-off; our town's did not. The blissfully convenient library? *It was no longer convenient.*

Then my children moved beyond awareness of their own hands and discovered the library. A quick trip to the front desk morphed into endless mornings of story hour, oogling the frogs in the fish tank, and reading every book in the children's section—six times over. Obtaining my beloved novels was now a COMMITMENT.

That was fine; I could handle this. I mean, yes, I would rather hide in the bathroom than sing another high-pitched version of "The Wheels on the Bus" with a bunch of toddlers, but hey, I'd signed up for this. I could do it. Plus I was pretty sure that hanging out in the library was good for young minds, a great way to develop educational skills or some such business. I got my books, they got smarter. Had to be a win-win, right?

In large part, we schooled the library together, which worked relatively well. Yet I'd be lying if I said I didn't covet solo trips to my book dealer. One day recently, feeling very schedule-smart, I swung down to the library to drop off some well-due items prior to preschool pick-up. I would drop my books without my kids even knowing I'd been there! Sneaky Mommy!

You can imagine my horror when I tugged on the library door to find it locked. My mind raced through the minor holidays; had they added a second President's Day of which I was unaware?   As I debated, my eyes landed on the sign, "Library closed. Has moved across from The Park." Cue stifled curses. What?!

In fairness, I had heard that the library was moving. Several months ago. Regardless, I feel like the township should have properly helped prepare me for the relocation by installing a flashing neon sign announcing the upcoming change.

In my front yard.

A month prior to the move.

And the directions "Across from The Park" proved especially challenging. Every other mother in my town knows where The Park is. I do not. This disqualifies me from being able to properly carry the title of "mom" in my town, I know.

It's not that I don't take my children to a park, because I do. I just don't take my children to *The Park*; we walk to the one closest to us instead. This works well for us, but when someone uses The Park as a directional reference or suggests, "Let's meet at The Park," it gets a little dicey. *It gets dicey because I don't actually know where The Park is.*

I have *found* The Park before. After an average of sixteen drive-bys, I can locate it. But it's not the kind of thing that happens without some extensive under-the-breath muttering.

And remember that perfectly timed preschool pick-up I had planned? *Yeah, it wasn't going to happen.*

Panicking for time, I started my drive-by procession. One drive-by, two drive-bys; by the time I hit five, I was pretty sure I was getting closer. The Park was definitely within reach. Getting there on time for my child, however, was not within reach.

I called my friend. You know *her*, the insanely responsible calm mom who would never get lost on her way to the library? While pleasantly agreeing to grab my daughter when she picked up her own son, she asked, "You don't know where The Park is?"

No, no I don't. And why yes, those are the scarlet letters TP on my head for "The Park."

Assured that my daughter was in far better hands than my incapable own, I resumed my drive-bys and by the grace of God, *actually managed to find The Park.* The only problem now was locating the freshly situated library. I parked and I searched. And searched.

There was NOTHING, excepting the lone fall-out-style bomb

shelter on the edge of the parking lot.

I called my husband and started to sob a bit, as I still had to scoot my way into the kindergarten pick-up line for my son ASAP. I searched, I prayed, I willed my eyes to see the glorious new building the township had poured my taxpayer dollars into. It was then that I finally, miraculously realized that *the fall-out shelter* was the library!

There were no signs. At all. God alone provided the tip-off that this was the building I'd been searching for. The parking resembled a nightmare scene of a dark one-way alley. Alone. At night. With many probable monsters lurking in the shadows. It was impossible to navigate the minivan through without hitting large amounts of elderly persons walking their teeny dogs in the vicinity of The Park.

Later, I would address the fact that our township directors were obviously vindictively attempting to thwart its citizens by hiding the library, but for now, *I was late.* I was furious. I called my husband again, desperate for sympathy. He empathetically responded, "I don't know why you are upset with me."

It was then that I suggested he spend his evening with the township planners slinging mud on the library building to further disguise its presence since they were all similarly in touch with what people really need and want on this Earth. *It may not have been one of my finer moments.*

Fast forward a half hour—books returned, children safely procured, friend profusely thanked—we all found ourselves at home. As I whipped up a batch of boxed macaroni bunnies (some days just call for them more than others), I reflected on how ridiculously hard kids make things.

What was to be a simple errand run threw me into the depths of impossibility and left me begging favors just to push through my day-to-day. But the darnedest thing was, *when I couldn't get to my kids when needed, I lost it.*

While I'd give my left arm for a peaceful library break, I don't think it's meant to be right now. I hope the future is packed full of such breaks along with lots of solitary bathroom time, but for now, I think the kids and I are rocking a group act. It's probably time to saddle up for a lot of team library runs, or accept that panicked scrambling will be part of any attempted solo ventures.

One for all and all for one? Something like that.

In the meantime, I made one final call to my husband. "We need to move," I told him. I cannot possibly be expected to function in a town that has such an ill-marked public library. The very idea is ludicrous.

MEREDITH SPIDEL blogs at The Mom of the Year where she dedicatedly earns her title one epic parenting fail at a time, offering quick, relatable laughs for fellow parents and all their empathizers. She has been part of several bestselling anthologies, featured on prominent sites such as The Huffington Post, In the Powder Room, and BlogHer, and loves her role as the Executive VP/Operations Manager of The BlogU Conference. When she's not breaking up fights over Legos and juice boxes, she remains fully committed to sharing a less serious look at the world of parenting.

How to Be a Terrible Mom
By Kim Bongiorno
Let Me Start By Saying

Everything I needed to know about being a terrible mom, I learned from my Nana.

She was a college-educated woman who fell in love with a man in Boston, and then fell in love with Vermont. They left the city and moved up north, had a daughter, and Nana used her degree to get her dream job: teaching in a one-room schoolhouse.

Suddenly, she found herself a widow. Knowing she had no other choice, she dried her tears and got to the business of raising her nine-year-old daughter alone. Five days a week she'd walk her daughter to the local elementary school, then get into the driver's seat of the school bus and go pick up the kids she taught in the poorer towns up by the mountains and bring them to her own little school. She worked hard, cared for many, gave her all to all of the children around her.

Years later, when her own daughter had a child, she gave up teaching to move in with her and help raise a beautiful grandson.

Her daughter ended up gaining three more kids by marriage, then having two more kids during that marriage, the last being me. I was brought up on three square meals a day, most made with ingredients fresh from the garden. Rather than work all day like Nana had, my mom stayed home. She baked, cleaned, volunteered at the schools. She folded fitted sheets properly and made sure we didn't watch too much television.

When it was my turn to be a mom, I took it all very seriously.

Before I had my first kid I stopped doing things for myself and instead spent months doing exhaustive research on diapers, swaddling, baby carriers, strollers, homemade baby food, breastfeeding, formula options, breast pumps, pacifiers, what to pack in my hospital bag, what kind of fabric his coming-home outfit should be, and everything else I could possibly find under the search term "baby" and "how not to screw up this parenting gig." I was thorough and efficient in my studying and planning.

I had to be The Best Mom Ever. My Nana sacrificed everything to raise my mom well. My mom was the traditional stay-at-home-mother who baked and cleaned and greeted the world with polite-ness and a smile, no matter how she was feeling. Wasn't it my turn to do the same now?

I had my son and *relished* in him. I was now a mother—a mother! He was my everything, and I would do as good a job as the women before me did—even if it killed me.

When he was three months old, I signed him up for more weekly classes than the average college freshman. I carried extra pacifiers with me in case I dropped one. I diced his fresh, home-cooked food into particles so small, it is a wonder no scientists approached me to work on splitting atoms in my free time. I bought organic and contin-ued my research and spoke in gentle words and focused on absolute-ly nothing but his health and happiness.

I tried to do it all "right."

I really did.

But then I had my second kid less than two years after my first, and all I could think about was who my Nana was after she was done with her child-rearing years.

Being the only living grandparent, Nana was the main babysitter when my parents went away. Everyone knew that each time she came to stay she'd have three suitcases: one with her clothes, one with lingerie, and one packed to the gills with candy. Us kids could have as much as we wanted, as long as we shared it with her.

She liked to cook but was terrible at it, so fed us frozen dinners and more ice cream than you could shake a stick at. She'd teach us card games, but not let us win every time. And when her beloved Red Sox were on television? We were not to be seen or heard. Nana would crack open a Budweiser, put her feet up in my father's chair, and yell smack at that television in a way that left my brother and I speechless.

Getting her to babysit was always a feat in the first place. She lived in an old lady apartment complex surrounded by other women who weren't ready to throw in the towel yet. They were constantly going on day trips to shop, gamble, whale-watch, or see up-and-coming comediennes. The woman's social calendar was packed, and Mom had to make sure to ask for her help way in advance.

Nana always dressed to impress, was never without her favorite coral-red lipstick on, and had a hearty laugh that made those of us around her laugh right along with her. She collected funny salt-and-pepper shakers on her travels, just because they made her happy, and she kept elephants with trunks-up in her home to surround herself with good luck. She was enjoying her life, being blissfully selfish, and loving every minute of it. Never feeling guilty about it, for it was finally time to balance out the giving and receiving in her life.

As I sat there with my two young kids, feeling the pressure of motherhood and housewifery in a way I never thought possible, I finally saw the parallels between my Nana and me up to that point. She and I both valued education, relished in being independent, fell in love in the big city, and moved to the suburbs to raise our family. I didn't want to give everything up that I enjoyed now, like she did, and just look forward to being as free as Nana was later in life. I decided that for people like her who never had the opportunity to enjoy parenthood and selfishness at the same time, I'd do the honors.

This decision finally made the Perfect Parent Pole fall right out of my ass, and that freedom was invigorating.

I wiped dropped pacifiers off on my shirt and popped them back into my kids' mouths. I let them eat cake—store bought cake! I had no energy to bake a damn thing. I stopped biting my tongue to try and make a good impression for the sake of my children, and instead let my sarcastic side show. I taught my kids how to play card games, and gleefully talked smack when I won. I invited kids over for my kids to play with, but also made sure to get out with my own friends, too.

I even tried wearing coral-red lipstick.

Sometimes my kids are ignored while I watch my own favorite television show; they have to miss a playdate because I'm away doing a job I love; or they pack their own lunches and tidy up their own beds. But I'm happier balancing the sacrifices I could make for them with the things I need to do for myself. And when I'm happier, everyone is happier.

So, sure, there are moms out there who might think I'm doing a bad job at parenting by allowing myself to be selfish, not making home-cooked meals all the time, or going out with my girlfriends instead of tucking my kids in at night. I'm okay with that. I think my Nana would have been, too.

She's the one I can credit with teaching me everything I needed to know about being a terrible mom. My only regret? I never got to thank her for it.

KIM BONGIORNO is an author, <u>freelance writer</u>, and the award-winning blogger behind <u>Let Me Start By Saying</u>. She lives in New Jersey with her handsome husband and two charmingly loud kids, who she pretends to listen to while playing on <u>Facebook</u> and <u>Twitter</u>. If she were less tired, she'd totally add something really clever to her bio so you'd never forget this moment.

Dusty Fake Flowers and Used Bras
By Stacia Ellermeier
Dried-on Milk

I love a good sale. I be poppin' tags at Goodwill and consignment shops all the time. However, I'm far too lazy to shop garage sales because unless it's a whole neighborhood having the sale, it's not worth my time to drive to a random house that has like three tables of dusty picture frames, candles, and fake flowers from 1963. It's not even retro cool, it's hoarder cool.

Every time I have a garage sale, by the time it's over I say I will never do another garage sale again. And then spring comes around, I look at my basement overflowing with kid toys and clothes and rather than burn the house down to take care of the cache, I do a garage sale. It's a vicious cycle. It's just that I can't justify taking all the perfectly good toys and clothes to Goodwill. So I think to myself that this will be the last garage sale, they aren't so bad. Boy howdy, I'm a dumb broad. Garage sales suck and it's the hardest three hundred dollars (if you're lucky) you'll ever make.

I looooove the moms who bring their kids garage sale shopping. Look, I'm a mom too. I have two littles. They are awesome and turds. Mostly turds when I want them to be awesome, like at a garage sale. I'm a hawk on their asses making sure they aren't stealing anything or putting parts of a toy in the shoe section. I try not to bring them but I realize that's not always possible. However, there are a lot of people who don't watch their kids at all, maybe they forgot they even brought their kids along, and those are the ones who visit my garage sales. "That little shit took a shoe! One shoe?! Why?"

During my garage sales my kids want to "help" but they just make my life so much harder:

"No, we can't buy that toy! We actually own it that toy. Not *another* toy, *that* toy that's in your hand is ours. I'm trying to sell it. Put it back."

"I know you want to handle the money but you are in kindergarten and do not know math. Like at all. Not even kind of a little bit. So no, you may not break change for a twenty."

"Oh, NOW you want to be Rapunzel. You never wanted to dress

up the two years we owned that dress because it itches."

The last sale kind of made me hate all of humanity so I might be done for at least a few years. There's nothing worse than walking into a stranger's garage to dig through piles of their junk and the whole time you're being watched by the owner. I like to think of it as my own little shop. I'm freaky organized. I'm a nerd. I know. I organize by sex and size. Toys are displayed nicely, all are tested beforehand to make sure they are working otherwise they go in the free box. Have you ever seen people's reactions to the free box? They go ape shit. OH MY GOD, A FREE WIRE HANGER!! It's like Black Friday at Walmart.

I decided I only had one day in me. Friday from eight to two. Dats it. That's all I got. Bring your little peddling shoes and buy my shit! I price to sell. Fiddy cents here, a quarter there and yet people STILL haggle on a candle half burnt down saying ten cents is too much. "How about a nickel?" they ask. How about you go fuck yourself and your nickel? How about that? I'm not sitting out here for my health, yo.

The day started out beautiful and then clouds started to form overhead. Oh hell, no you didn't, Mother Nature! Oh yes, she did. That bitch brought a nice little rain storm that lasted about an hour that morning. I had to drag everything into the garage or under the pop up tent. Oh yes, I had a pop up tent and it was rad. I know how to throw a good-ass garage sale. The tent only blew over about six times and I used about four hundred cuss words but it was worth it!

The hardcore garage salers weren't deterred by the storm. They smashed their bodies into my tiny garage and shopped their hearts out. The only problem with having a garage sale inside your garage is that people ask if nearly everything in the garage is for sale. Like ya know, all that stuff behind that sheet you put up to keep people from thinking that stuff is for sale … is that for sale? Oh and while I'm on a stupid streak, is your patio set that's on your patio, that's no where near the stuff for sale … is that for sale, too? Actually is your house for sale? Because I'll offer you fifty bucks! Or better yet, I know you did all this work, set things up nicely, and tag everything but I'm going to go ahead and make a huge mound of clothes and toys total-ing sixty-five dollars and offer you fifteen dollars because we both know you don't want to put all the shit back.

What a bunch of dickwads.

The storm passed and the rest of the day turned out to be pretty nice, but that also meant the freak shows were coming out of the woodworks because garage sale. I was selling an eight hundred dol-lar camcorder for a fiver. Everything was there, the cords, the manu-al, the case, except the stupid power cord. I couldn't find it but it was a universal thingy, easy enough to find at the store. Five dollars was a steal and this motherfucker offered me three bucks. O.K. fine, we can haggle but since it was still early in the day I said no. I wanted a solid five dollars.

He said, "But it's missing the power cord." Oh right, that. Still man, it's five dollars!

I finally caved and said, "Fine, three." I'm such a pushover. An-other guy overheard this conversation, stepped in, and said he'd give me five dollars for the camera. I said O.K.! You win! The three dollar guy clutched that camcorder like this was a famine and that was the last piece of bread on Earth. He said, "NO! You said three dollars. I had it first. I buy it for three." Yo. Shit just got real up in here! I was all, "Yeeeeah you just give me three dollars and walk your little ass right off my driveway ... mmmkay?"

Things started to slow down around lunch time and the hubs came out to see how it was going. Right then this lady parked her gi-normous van in our driveway. Um. Listen, that's not reserved park-ing spot just for you ... because we are having a garage sale ... which means people don't park on the driveway where the garage sale is taking place ... I just ... da fuck? This lady hops out and starts poking around inside the garage. Jason, the hubs, and I are talking, not really paying attention to her. After a few minutes the lady says to Jason, "I'm going to need you to go inside because my daughter wants to come in here and look around but she's in her PJs and you can't see her like that." Jason looks at me and then to her and back to me. I just shrugged and he went inside. God damn weirdos! Her daughter, who looks about twentyish, came into the garage all wrapped up in a blanket like she was hibernating in it. Turns out she had no clothes on. Not a stitch of fabric on her body other than the blanket that kept blowing open. Ask me how I know. Images you can't unsee.

After the peep show, I was blessed by a lady haggling over a twenty dollar bike. She offered me a ten and I accepted. Fine, whatever. I was getting close to closing up shop and I didn't care anymore. I just wanted the shit gone. She said she needed to run home to get the money and asked if I would hold the bike. O.K., but I'm closing in an hour, you betta get your ass back here quickly. Dat bitch didn't come back for FIVE HOURS!! She rang our doorbell at like nine o'clock that night saying she had the ten dollars for the bike. I'm not even going to ask what you had to do to get that ten dollars and let me put on an Ove' Glove before I take that bill from you. Yes, I still took the money and she got her rusty old bike. I just made sure to dip the bill in bleach before it touched anything on my person.

Did you know people buy used bras? Yup. They will also buy power tools from 1976 and bed pillows and old stained Tupperware. But alas, I can't rag on people who buy used bras or dusty fake flowers. To each their own. I think I'll stick to waiting another couple years before I get a bug up my ass and do another garage sale thinking I'll make some decent money and end up with seventy-five dollars for all my efforts. They are exhausting and I don't enjoy talking to strangers that much. Garage salers are a special breed, that's fo sho.

STACIA ELLERMEIER is a graphic designer who moonlights as a parenting-humor writer on her blog, __Dried-on Milk__*. She finds inspiration in her two littles, husband, and a cat who barfs on everything. She's known for running over the orange directional cones at her daughter's school and her extreme skills of self-embarrassment. Stacia was a Top 4 finalist in Blogger Idol 2013 and can be found spewing verbal diarrhea on NickMom and Erma Bombeck's Writer's Workshop. She loves chapstick, books, Starbucks and Target. Follow Stacia on Facebook, Pinterest, Twitter, Google+ or Instagram.*

That Time I Went to Target by Myself
By Jennifer Hicks
Real Life Parenting

It was a rare moment in time that had me in a state of euphoric bliss—I was walking the aisles of Target all by myself. No children asking to see the toys. No one telling me they had to pee when we were at the farthest corner of the store. Nobody complaining because they alternately wanted to *waaaaaaaaalk*, but then were so *tiiiiiiiired* they wanted to ride. It was just me, free as a bird, drunk off of my own freedom.

I walked up and down each and every aisle in the store simply because I could. I stopped to look at everything I wanted to see. I spent five entire minutes looking at toothpaste. *When did they come out with so many flavors and varieties? Berry Mint? Orange Zest and Rosemary??* I had become so accustomed to the Grab and Go method of time-efficient shopping that I realized I hadn't stood and looked at all the options available to me in the field of dental care.

It was exhilarating.

As I rounded the next corner, I saw an end cap gleaming with a red sale sign. *Well, if it's on sale, I should check it out,* I thought. *It's clearly the responsible thing to do.*

I have no recollection of anything else on those shelves that day, but I can tell you what caught my eye. It was a box of Self-Warming Wax Strips for "Salon quality smooth skin in the comfort of your own home."

I absolutely loathe shaving my lady garden. The razor burn, the prickly stubble, the ingrown hairs. I wanted a better solution—and there, with the red bullseye beckoning me like a siren calling my cart to listen to her hair removal song, was the answer to my pubic prayers: No Muss, No Fuss Self-Warming Wax Strips (Perfect for the Bikini Region). For a mere three dollars and eighty-nine cents I could rid my nether regions of unwanted hair with "easy to use" strips and save myself the troubles of shaving and the embarrassment of having someone else involved with ripping hair out of my fur taco. I was intrigued. "No muss, no fuss." I liked the sound of that. *Besides, it was a veritable bargain, it would be more costly NOT to buy these based on this great deal!*

These were the kinds of decisions I was making in my fully ine-briated state of Mother Shopping Sans Children.

The next morning, while my kids were comatose in front of the television watching educational programming, I decided to get busy with my new purchase. Having never waxed a thing in my life, I made sure to read the back of the box carefully:

1. Hair to be removed must be 1/8" or longer. *Uh, nooooo prob-lem. The shrubbery was in full bloom.*

2. Take one strip and remove shiny layer of plastic. *This is so easy. They were right about that!*

3. Place wax directly onto section of hair to be removed. *Let's just hoick the leg up onto the sink so I have a better view of the jun-gle down under ... and, boom. Look at me: waxing like a boss!*

4. Allow body heat to warm wax strip for one to two minutes. *Okeedokee! I might as well put my leg down while I'm waiting for this to wa—JESUS CHRIST ON A CRUTCH!! Ouch! Ow! Pulling the hairs! Pulling. All. The. Hairs. So, nope. I'm just gonna leave my leg up here on the sink while I wait.*

5. When wax is warm, remove strip with a very rapid motion against the hair growth while keeping the skin taut with the other hand. *Wait. What?? I don't know which direction these hairs grow. Out. They grow OUT. That's all I know. O.K. 'Pulling the skin taut.' What does THAT mean?? I don't know so I'm just gonna skip that. All right, let's just give this a whirl. One, two, threeeee! HOLY FIRE ON MY FORTUNE COOKIE! Ow! Ow! Owowowowowowow! Good gravy that hurts like a MoFo!*

After about thirty seconds of Lamaze breathing to get me through the pain, the stars were no longer dominating my vision. So I looked at the Tool of Torture in my hand expecting to see a very hairy strip of wax. To my complete disappointment and absolute sur-prise, there were NO pubes on that strip. Not a single one. And, upon closer inspection, I also noticed there was no wax on that piece of cloth. *What the—? How in the—? Where in the—?*

And then I took my foot off the sink and had an instant surge of pain pulling my thoughts straight back to my Chia Pet. I looked down and saw the thick, sticky wax strip matted into my twilight zone. *This doesn't seem right. I think the wax was supposed to stay on the paper. I mean, I'm no professional, but this really seems like the wax should NOT be caked in my undercarriage.*

I tried to peel the wax out but quickly found that those short and curlies were like little corkscrews holding onto that wax as if their hairy lives depended on it.

Code Glue! Holy hell! I can see it now: 'Jennifer Hicks died unexpectedly at home from complications in a painful pubic hair removal catastrophe. She was found unresponsive on the floor of her bathroom clutching a box of No Muss, No Fuss Self-Warming Wax Strips.'

As I was lost in the thought of being found in a heap on my bathroom floor, I was yanked back to reality by an excruciating pull of my lady mane. I knew I had to figure something out. I refused to die in a tragic home waxing accident.

Maybe if I get it really warm, it will just turn to liquid and melt off. That has to work. Seriously, it HAS to work!

I ran hot water in the bathtub. In my absolute desperation to find relief, I almost immediately climbed into the tub to begin Operation Get This Shit Off of My Lady Bits. I lowered myself in and sat down. The water was almost too hot to sit in, but I was certain that would be the lesser of the many evils ravaging my bathing suit region.

I was wrong.

I leaned forward to adjust the water temperature and I quickly found that the wax was not only stuck to my furby, it was also stuck to the bottom of the tub. The only thing that I had been effectively able to accomplish was affixing myself to the floor of my bathtub.

By my vagina.

I was like that construction worker in the super glue commercial whose hard hat was stuck to a steel beam as he dangled in the air swinging his legs back and forth except I was stuck by my sweet spot to the bathtub not daring to move a muscle. As I began to envision my newly updated obituary, my sweet three-year-old daughter came bounding into the bathroom.

I Still Just Want to Pee Alone

"Hi, Mommy! Are you takin' a baff?"

Keeping my gaze focused straight ahead, I managed to grunt out a simple "Mmmhmm."

"Oooooh, I love baffs. Baffs are so fun. Do you want bubbles in your baff? I love bubbles. I can take a baff wiff you, Mommy? We can take a bubble baff togever!"

Before I could respond, she turned to open the cupboard where I kept the bubble bath but was distracted by the paraphernalia on the sink.

"What's dis stuff, Mommy? Is it new makeup? What's dis box wiff the lady's legs on it?"

"It's a big mistake. That's what it is."

I wanted to say: *It's the worst three dollars and eighty-nine cents I've ever spent and I swear to all that's good and holy I won't let you make this same error in judgment when you're a grown woman.*

Instead I said, "Can you please go get Mommy the phone?"

I need to call 1-800-HOW-DO-I-GET-THIS-OUTTA-MY-MUFF??

'No Muss, No Fuss' my ass.

JENNIFER HICKS is the writer behind <u>Real Life Parenting</u>. With sass, smarts, and a big mouth, she keeps it real, oftentimes writing what most people think but are afraid to say out loud. She writes about the good, the bad, the ugly, and sometimes the very funny in life and parenting. She's been featured on BonBon Break, Mamapedia, Erma Bombeck Writers' Workshop, and went viral on The Huffington Post with her piece "<u>Dear Mom on the iPhone: You're Doing Fine</u>." You can find her inspired hashtags and famous #SelfiesThatEmbarrassYourTeen on <u>Facebook</u>, <u>Twitter</u>, <u>Pinterest</u>, and <u>Instagram</u>.

One Versus Many
By Tracy DeBlois
Orange & Silver

I have four children, three boys and a girl, who are in the stage our society calls pre-adolescent or tween. I often wonder if I'm qualified to parent them. Most parents have a certain mistrust of their abilities, of course, but I was an only child. I have a hard time relating to my kids' sibling conflicts because I have no firsthand knowledge of them. Even for the general childhood experiences we share, almost all of theirs are colored by their sibling interactions, which mine weren't. I didn't have brothers and sisters to fight with, call me fat and ugly, and reminded me that I was socially awkward; I had to develop poor self-esteem and anxiety disorders on my own.

My husband has a brother, so often he's better at managing things than I am. And by "things" I mean, for example, events that sound like Grand Central Station on the Friday evening before Memorial Day weekend. Except at our house, we call that "bedtime." Although he's more tolerant of chaos than I am, he does have his limits—after all, we have twice as many kids as he grew up with.

Still, he's better at overlooking some of what whips me into a frenzy. Take the arguing. It's not that I didn't argue with my friends, but our disputes were over important things, like whose Barbie got to date Ken, and who had to settle for the short, less handsome, sensitive-looking dad from The Sunshine Family. My kids fight about shit like the order in which the *Hunger Games* movies are coming out (hint: the same order as the books, the last one split into two movies called "Part 1" and "Part 2"—why is this something to fight about?), if there's a difference between a journal and a diary, and (I swear I'm not making this up) you're trying to touch me with the calculator that was in your underwear. WTF?

Some disagreements are easy to settle, but sometimes the conflict is over something that's legitimately shared, like whose turn it is to pick the television show. I hate this debate because I'm completely torn. They're all my children; I want them all to have what they want. I tell them, "If you can't sort it out and stop fighting, the television goes off." This usually works, so I'm assuming it's the right thing to do, but maybe all my kids are being mentally scarred because I refuse to settle the argument about whether they should watch *Austin & Ally* or *Lab Rats*.

Only children don't understand the appeal of annoying noises. Sometimes when my kids are playing in another room one of them will decide to start saying something like, "Derp." He'll say it maybe half a dozen times, in a slow, measured pace: "Derp … derp … derp … derp … " after about the fifth repetition, one of them will say, "STOP IT!" Oh, shit gets real then. I know I'm not going to hear anything for the next twenty minutes except one kid saying, "Derp … derp … " and one kid yelling, "STOP IT!" every forty-five seconds.

My husband tells me to ignore this, but it's hard for me. I'm not used to constant bickering. When you're an only child, if you make a strange noise while you're playing in your room, no one cares, and there's no one to annoy you in a like fashion. I'm not conditioned to ignore either the repetitive noise, or the perpetual attempts to silence it.

My own childhood didn't prepare me for the challenge of getting four kids to perform basic acts of hygiene. Tooth brushing is the least of it. There's also bathing or showering, underwear changing, and hair brushing. Right now my kids are young enough not to care about the opposite sex, so I'm hopeful that when they do discover their chromosomal opposites they'll take more interest in this aspect of their upkeep, even though I realize that may mean there could be three people in my house who smell like the entire Axe body spray display. (I like to think my daughter will pick something other than Axe.)

The hardest part for me is the physical fighting. Only children don't get into wrestling matches with other kids—well, I didn't, possibly because I was a girl, as well as an only. Maybe boys are more inclined? Still, I never roughhoused with my friends the way my kids do with each other. When the fight is a genuine conflict, I have to put a stop to it (not that that's easy to do) because sometimes they threaten to get so violent I worry I should hide the baseball bats and claw hammers, but sometimes it's because they're excited. Then there's a lot of picking up and pushing around, which isn't always welcome by the recipient, and they dissolve into a battle.

This is foreign to me; I remember when I was a child my mother expressing a concern that I never seemed to get very excited about anything. She was wrong, of course. I just didn't outwardly express it. My kids have no such inhibitions.

Beyond the basics of keeping them clean, and safe from bodily harm at the hands of one another, there are some more nuanced difficulties that have presented themselves, which are not exclusive to my children, but I'm a bit uncertain what strategy to use to deal with them. I think of these as "sex and Santa" issues. That is, how to keep the older one(s) from sharing information or knowledge that comes with maturity (a term I use loosely with my children) with younger siblings who don't need to know these things. It will soon be a moot point; the youngest will be there in a couple of years, but right now I do a lot of abrupt subject changing.

The real skill, the one I assume I would have learned if my mother had more than one child, is the ability to tailor my parenting style to suit the child. As it is, I have a single style—the one my mother used with me—in which I set unreasonable expectations and yell when my expectations aren't met. Perhaps the belief that I would be aware enough as a kid to pick up on the difference in her parenting style with me versus my sibling(s) is in itself an unreasonable expectation. Considering that an Internet search for "tailor parenting style to fit the child" brought up over twenty-four million results, clearly I'm not alone in my uncertainty about this. I think the theory I've been using so far is the one I'll have to stick with: that which does not kill them gives them something to discuss with their therapist in twenty years. Come to think of it, that may have been my mom's theory, too.

I Still Just Want to Pee Alone

TRACY DEBLOIS has a husband, four children, a dog, and a full time job. Her work has appeared on the Erma Bombeck Writers' Workshop website and Ten to Twenty Parenting. She blogs at Orange & Silver, providing a humorous glimpse into the never-settling snow globe that is her mind. Her days are spent answering questions about the location of her children's belongings, figuring out what's for dinner, and reminding everyone that socks without feet in them do not belong in the living room. She can be found at **Orange & Silver Blog** *and on Facebook and Twitter.*

Baby Monitors: A Cautionary Tale
By Victoria Fedden
Wide Lawns and Narrow Minds

I don't know how I went almost a year without a baby monitor, but it probably had something to do with the fact that I was a terrible parent. I didn't have a baby wipe warmer or a Diaper Genie either. I didn't take my two-month-old infant to any Mommy & Me glockenspiel classes and my kid's stroller came from the Goodwill, so I guess it makes sense that I went without the monitor too. And yes, in eighteen years if my daughter ends up wrapped around a metal pole wearing five inch, Lucite heels and calling herself "Lush'ysse" you can blame it on how deprived she was as a newborn.

The funny thing is, I *had* a monitor. I just couldn't figure the damned thing out. It was one of those fancy video monitors that my friend who has a big trust fund got for my shower. It was an impressive gift for sure and I definitely intended to use it because seriously, how cool would it be to sit for hours on end and watch a three inch screen of a sleeping baby in grainy, greenish night vision? Umm, not really. That actually sounded kind of creepy and with my luck I'd probably end up recording unwanted paranormal activity and then we'd have to move and call an exorcist and it would be so inconvenient and that just sounded like a hassle, so I pretty much gave up trying to get the video monitor to work. When people asked me why I wasn't using it I'd just be like: "Demons. Poltergeists. I'd rather not know, you know?" And then they'd ask me if I was still on my psych meds, which I was not.

Not wanting my friend's gift to go to waste, I put in a valiant effort at trying to get the video monitor to work. I did an Internet search for instructions. I watched videos. I had my husband mess with it and naturally he *was* able to get it to work, because he is a man, but then as soon as he'd leave, the device would go black and refuse to operate until he returned. Further proof of my poltergeist theory right there. I imagined the demons in my house laughing their asses off at how they were fucking with my technology.

"Dude, let's make it always work for her husband but never for her! She'll go insane!" I imagined them laughing uproariously.

I Still Just Want to Pee Alone

So I gave up on the whole video monitor thing for a while because my house was small and I could hear the baby, plus I was too busy keeping her alive to fool with it. Then a few months later bad mother guilt got to me and I realized that it might actually be very pleasant to sit in the porch or go out in the yard once in a while when the baby was asleep so I went to Walmart and bought myself a seventeen dollar basic non-video baby monitor and my entire life changed for the better. Arguably.

Just as I feared, my house really was demon possessed. By a ghost baby. Over and over I'd hear the ghost baby, who apparently had colic or something, shrieking to high heaven. I'd run in to my baby's room and find her curled peacefully, dreaming in her crib while the ghost baby wailed on. Then one day I heard the ghost baby's mom comforting her through the monitor and I figured it out. No, it was not an entire ghost family. It was the neighbors. They had a baby too. Their monitor was set on the same channel as mine and our houses were close enough that when I turned the monitor on, I essentially had them under surveillance. Which was kind of cool, except that their baby cried all the time and they were boring. For a while I tried to entertain myself by listening to them through the monitor but alas, they were not Russian spies or swingers or anything else that might have been exciting to overhear, so I gave up and switched my monitor to Channel B, thus ceasing further eavesdropping.

I soon realized that the baby monitor could also come with the potential for embarrassment. Not only could I hear my neighbors, but it also occurred to me that they could hear us too, which explains why they starting snickering and winking at me after that night I accidentally left the monitor in my bedroom and not the baby's. Jeez. It was our anniversary! We were trying something new, I mean, *never mind*! It was the television! We were watching HBO. I swear. Those shows get crazy.

Then, take for instance, this other situation, which it is important to remember is purely hypothetical. Remember that—*hypothetical*.

Imagine your joy at just having discovered the new freedoms afforded by the baby monitor. Say you're just so happy that you take it with you to a party with lots of people you admire and you're really excited about attending and then let's say that your baby goes to sleep in the guest room in her pack n play and you get the baby monitor all hooked up so you can go back to the party and have a grand old time while the baby sleeps and you are just so pleased with yourself. You didn't need a babysitter or anything.

Perhaps in an hour or so your baby wakes up and cries and you hear it on the baby monitor you are so excited about and you rush off to comfort her, or, umm, *him* as the case may be and then let's say that in your haste you forgot the receiving end of the monitor on the dinner table where my, I mean *your*, friends are still lingering after dinner enjoying coffee and dessert.

Here is my advice to you if you find yourself in this again, *hypothetical* situation which I'm not saying actually happened to me, although it could have. Maybe.

Take the receiver with you because you might end up going into the bedroom to get the baby and then finding that all of a sudden out of nowhere you have to poop and you might thank God that the bedroom has a bathroom attached and that the baby can see you on the toilet from the pack n play. And if the baby cries and fusses while you are on the toilet, please, please don't start making up a song that may or may not go "Mommy is Pooping! Pooping Mommy! Poo Poo Mommy Poo Poo Poo!"

Because once you finish and get the baby settled back down and you are ready to rejoin the dinner party, when you return to the table you may be met with an awkward silence. Your friends may appear to be trying very hard not to laugh. Others may not be able to make eye contact with you. One of them might even call and sing the "Poo Poo Mommy" song on your voice mail the next day. Someone else might post the lyrics to your Facebook wall. You might forever be nicknamed "Pooping Mommy" by your group of loving companions.

And again, I'm not saying this happened to me. I just want to make sure that it doesn't happen to you. Just in case. That's all I'm trying to do.

VICTORIA FEDDEN is a writer and a mom from Fort Lauderdale, Florida. She writes to let people know that we're all crazy and that we're going to be okay anyway. She's the author of the memoirs Amateur Night at the Bubblegum Kittikat *and* Sun Shower: Magic, Forgiveness and How I Learned to Bloom Where I Was Planted, *and blogs at* her website *about books, writing, bad recipes and life in South Florida. Her writing has appeared in Real Simple, Chicken Soup for the Soul, The Huffington Post, Scary Mommy and various publications. Please visit her* Facebook page *for updates.*

Betty Crock-of-Shit
By Mackenzie Cheeseman
Is there cheese in it?

I'm not trying to be dramatic or anything, but deciding what to make for dinner every night, and then actually preparing it, sort of makes me want to die.

See, I'm not the best cook. I mean, I can make a couple of decent dishes for potlucks or whatever, but for the most part, it's just not my strong suit. And even the stuff I can cook takes forever. Like, you know how recipes say "Prep Time?" Well, multiply that by about seven and that's how long it takes me. Once at preschool, Jack's teacher told him he probably better not have a snack because I would be there to pick him up soon, and then it would be dinner time. His response? "I should *definitely* have a snack now, because my mom cooks willy, willy slow." It also doesn't help that no matter what I make, they don't eat it. Every meal is like a nuclear standoff, and I'm ready to fry myself in a boiling vat of Smart Balance by the time we're through.

I actually used to sort of enjoy cooking, every once in a while, when there were no rabid koalas banging on the table, screeching for dinner, and threatening me with blunt objects. I also loved baking. I would make cookies and cupcakes and sundry sweets-on-sticks all the time. I'd get more points for presentation than flavor, but whatever, you can't win 'em all.

But I have seriously lost my mojo. Every afternoon, around three, I feel this impending sense of doom. It's like a black cloud that creeps over me and starts to crush my soul. What in the hell is for dinner? That's probably half the battle right there.

I would like to give a shout-out to my husband because he does probably eighty percent of the grocery shopping, which I HATE. Seriously, I am such an ineffective shopper. I go so infrequently I don't really know where anything is and I end up making ninety-three laps of the whole damn store and still I come home with seven different types of bread and an ice cream sandwich sampler platter, but failed to purchase the ONE essential item I actually went to the market for. (The Hubs usually even takes the kids with him to shop. Score!

Sorry ladies, you can't have him, he's all mine!)

And lately, I guess because I am so woefully pathetic at my wifely duties, he's started buying semi-prepared meals, and writing up a weekly meal plan for me. I mean, I know I'm not painting myself as a very sympathetic victim right now, but I'm just being honest. Even with all this help from my amazing husband, I absolutely dread making dinner. At this point I'm totally in my own head about it and things that aren't even that hard seem impossible. "Ugh, I have to cook the spaghetti *and* put butter on it?! Just kill me now."

Last year I had this big idea to start an herb garden. Made total sense. You know, because I used basil that one time. Needless to say, the herb garden is mostly dead. Except for one sad midget jalapeño, and the rosemary, which is some freak mutant variety that grew from a fledgling little plant into basically a tree despite my best attempts to murder it. (Well, it *was* doing well, until our new puppy, Feta, basically ate the thing and has now been depositing herb-infused dog shit all over our yard. How very Martha Stewart of her.)

Anyway. This weekend I was telling my husband we should try to reinvigorate the herbs and he said, "Yeah, actually, when my mom was here she was saying we should try vegetables instead. Like cucumbers. Since, y'know, you don't really cook anyway, so it's not like you need a bunch of fancy herbs." I totally got my panties in a rumple and I was like, "I cook *every single day*. Okay. Fine. Five days a week. That's a lot, goddammit."

He knew better than to say anything, but I could read his raised eyebrows loud and clear: "'Cook' is a generous term for what you do."

That fucker.

He's right, though. Really, most of what I do could be more aptly characterized as "reheating." Yeah, and "ordering." You're definitely not winning at life when the pizza guy knows you by name. "Hey, Mackenzie! You're calling on a Thursday! That's new. Are you still going to want pizza on Sunday as well? Wow, jalapeños, huh? Spicing it up tonight! Are you sure you want a large salad, ma'am? Do you have company or something, because you usually get the small."

Still. Hit me where it hurts. Geez. What is it about the (in)ability to put a warm, nutritious meal on the table that gets you right in your mom balls? It just seems like it's one of the most basic, essential duties as a mother/parent, and I sorta suck at it.

I wish Wolfgang Puck was my fairy godmother.

Or even Rachael Ray.

Really, any fairy that can cook a decent meal would do. I'm not picky. (But my kids are.)

MACKENZIE CHEESEMAN, a.k.a. Mack N. Cheese (not her real name, you'll be shocked to hear), is a mother, wife, lawyer, Google doctor, terrible chef, lazy laundress, community snot rag, compulsory snuggle sheriff, ambassador of arachnid amnesty, and crafty mo-fo. She likes beaches, books, booze and bad words. She lives in San Diego with her two children, Colby and Jack, or four, if you count Daddy Mack, the overgrown man-child that is her husband, and their pup Feta, who has expensive taste in shoes (to eat, not wear). When she's not doing those other things, she writes a blog at http://istherecheeseinit.blogspot.com/.

Deal
By Keesha Beckford
Mom's New Stage

At four o'clock on the Friday afternoon before Memorial Day weekend, I was all set to kick off summer. I was in my car, just three blocks away from home, when my phone rang. It was the call I'd been waiting for.

Back in January, I had applied for a position teaching dance at a local swanky private school. It was a big-girl job that would have meant a significant pay raise, and proved to all the world that I could work full-time and remain a halfway decent mother and wife. After interviewing with everyone at the school, and teaching an awesome audition class, I made it down to one of the three finalists. By the end of May, I would have killed for an answer—the answer I was about to get.

"Hello?" I was practically panting. It was Mr. So-and-So, the department head, asking if this was a good time. I told him I was driving, but that I was almost home.

"Duooooooooh, boy," Mr. So-and-so sighed. I tried to tell him I'd pull over, but he seemed convinced that, in my sorrow, I'd wrap my car around a tree. He agreed to call me back in ten.

I knew this was bad. Super bad. But maybe there was still a chance?

Ten minutes later I was given the standard compliments and thanked for my time.

And eleven minutes and thirteen seconds later, I had strapped on every piece of emotional baggage I owned and was trudging through the lands of "They-didn't-want-me!"; "How-could-they-not-want-ME?!"; "Fuck-them-with-flagpoles-for-not-wanting-me!"; and "No-one-will ever-want me again."

Later, I threw myself a raging pity party. I drank multiple glasses of wine. I had ice cream and cookies for dinner. I snapped at my children. Then, feeling guilty, I broke down sobbing in front of them and explained why I was so sad. Their eyes widened before asking, "So, can *we* have some ice cream?" Because I was clearly raising sociopaths, I cried harder. The condolences and encouragement I solicited from my Facebook entourage felt like big, fat lies, and I could only snivel through heart-to-heart chats with my besties and husband.

Although I barely slept that night, I thought I'd wake up Saturday morning with a brand new outlook on life. But I would have had more success sprinting away from a case of chocolate chip cookie dough sleeves than crawling out of the deep, dark funk I was in. When my daughter's non-washable marker went through her paper and on to our already "distressed" dining room table, it only served as further evidence that the universe was using me as its personal colostomy bag. I was in that horrible place where every mishap cackled in my face and told me what a hot mess I was. Like a petulant tween, I ran to my room, hurled myself onto my bed, and ugly-cried.

By early afternoon, however, I decided to put on my big-girl panties and deal. It was a gorgeous day, and taking my little guy and gal to the park was a perfect distraction.

I'd been pushing my kids on the swings and watching them navigate the jungle gym for around twenty minutes, when my four-year-old announced, "I have to go to the bathroom."

"Oh, come on!" I barked. I was pissed because I knew this would happen. I had practically gotten down on my hands and knees and begged her to go before we left, but my little darling had adamantly refused. "Can't you just wait five minutes until we can walk back home?" I asked. Her whining and grimacing told me all I needed to know.

I pulled my little lady behind the sturdiest tree I cold find and whipped down her underpants. Not only that, but I held her hands so she could squat low and back, to keep the stream away from her underwear. For someone who had to go so urgently, things were awfully quiet. Staring at the space between her undercarriage and the ground, I waited and waited.

Then, with stealthy precision, a sausage-like tube slithered downward and plopped in the dirt. *What the … ? This was too much!* I couldn't land a job. My children clamored for dessert while their mother sobbed inconsolably. And I had given birth to a beautiful daughter who shat behind trees like a cocker spaniel hopped up on prune juice.

"Oh my God! Oh my God! Number TWO? I thought you meant number one! Seriously? We have to go home right now!"

"I told you I had to go!" my little one cried. "I couldn't help it!"

Would something like this happen when I came to the park armed with tissues, wipes, hand sanitizer and maybe even one of those nifty freestanding toilet seats equipped with its own deodorized bag? (Yes, people! They really make those things!) No. It had to happen the one day I traveled light, with only my ID, keys, phone, and a few dollars. The woman who shook her fists and all but tackled folks who didn't pick up after their dogs was now leaving a bratwurst-sized turd in a popular neighborhood park.

Shamed and humiliated, my little girl wailed with the injustice of it all. Of course she did. What else could you do when your mother, the person who was supposed to have your back, turned into a screaming nut-job and made you feel like crap?

I bent down and hugged my daughter, begging her forgiveness by saying "I'm sorry" over and over again. If I could have beaten myself with a scourge I would have.

We gathered our things and went home to clean up, change clothes, and to fetch a wad of paper towels and plastic bags for poop scooping.

A half hour later, my kids were back playing at the park, while I used four hundred and seventy-eight sheets of paper towel to pick up our little deposit without one single poopi-cule touching my hand. As my bag of filth landed in the trashcan with a loud "thunk!" I finally smiled.

My daughter was the messenger, and it couldn't have been timelier.

Shit happens.

It was no longer a metaphor. It was real. And it was miraculous! For the last thirty years I had been searching for a way to believe that I wasn't being punished for a horrible crime in a past life, nor was I an unworthy failure of a person—sometimes I was just a victim of bad luck. Nothing else had made me see that no matter how pretty and smart and diligent and organized I might have been, some things were just plain out of my control.

No longer did I have to bat around an empty cliché to soothe myself when things went wrong. I now had a kick-ass visual! Sure, it would have been nice to have an image that had nothing to do with a little girl dropping a log in public. But that shit worked magic, so it was a keeper.

Before her two children re-choreographed her life, KEESHA BECKFORD was a professional dancer who performed in the U.S. and in Europe. Today she teaches dance in Chicago. She is also the cyclone behind the blog Mom's New Stage. A multitasker at heart, she has mastered simultaneously writing, choreographing, checking social media updates, playing the role of a mother named Joan "Kumbaya" Crawford, and burning food. Keesha is an editor at BonBonBreak.com whose writing has been featured on The Huffington Post, Mamapedia, What the Flicka, and in the bestselling anthologies I Just Want to Pee Alone *and* "You Have Lipstick on Your Teeth."

Officially on Top of Things
By Vicki Lesage
Life, Love, and Sarcasm in Paris

Women hate me yet envy me at the same time. "How does she do it?" they ask, as I cross the last item off my to-do list and plop down on the couch to watch television in my perfectly clean house.

I am a neat-freak. My to-do list is always under control. I am Officially on Top of Things.

Oh wait.

Those should all be past tense.

None of this is true now that I have two kids.

With the arrival of the first bundle of joy, my son, I was still doing pretty O.K. Not great, not horrible. Just pretty O.K.

There was that time I put "lotion" on my dry, cracked hands for days, only to discover I'd been using soap. I could *possibly* blame that on the language barrier. You see, despite living in France for ten years I'm still an idiot when it comes to simple translations like "hand cream." In my defense, the bottle had the word "milk" on it, which seems to imply more of a lotion-y substance than a soapy substance. One could argue that the word "milk" has no place on a lotion OR soap bottle, and one would probably be right. The French are weird.

For the most part, I was still Officially on Top of Things with this sweet little baby in our house. I had Baby Brain, but not a bad case of it. My house was still tidy enough to eat off the floor—if you had low enough standards.

Then the stork brought another baby, my daughter, and all bets were off. On her own, my daughter was an easy baby. But paired with her two-year-old brother, they became the neediest needers who needed. My tired brain and body couldn't take it.

I lumbered around in a daze, breathing out of my open mouth like the Neanderthal I'd become. It's possible I drooled in public. I don't know. I can't remember. Brain cells died by the minute, and they weren't being replaced.

Then I had the brilliant idea to return to work. Actually, I had the brilliant idea to help pay the bills, so I had to return to work.

On top of caring for two kids and trying in vain to keep the house clean, I now worked full-time and commuted a solid hour each way.

The transformation to full-on zombie was under way.

My first month back at work, I got hit with a nasty cold. "Cold? Puh-lease," I said with a snort. "I can handle this." (Actually, I didn't snort because I don't know how. Could someone teach me? That would really come in handy when reading books about farm animals to my kids. Right now, my horses and pigs sound like drunk drag queens.)

Then the cold turned into bronchitis. "Bronchitis? O.K., I admit, this one's a little tougher. But I've got this under control." (Now my drunken drag queens had sexy, raspy voices. I can't decide if that made it better or worse, but I'm pretty sure the answer is WAY WORSE.)

Then one day at work, I was rushing from department to department, trying to fix a problem on our website. Don't ask me why I was rushing. I work in a French office where the only time you'll see someone hurry is if they're late for their three-hour lunch, and even then you'll only get a tiny hustle out of them. After all, they still need time for a smoke on the walk over.

So there was no pressure from my colleagues to hurry. There shouldn't have even been pressure from myself. I know I'm a hard worker. I don't need to run around to prove it. And my bronchitis-encumbered lungs didn't need any extra exertion.

Yet there I was, firing on one cylinder at best, trying to prove to the world that I was still Officially on Top of Things. Armed with the information I needed to resolve the issue, after meeting with the head of production in our printing facility downstairs, I dashed upstairs to my desk. Except in my exhausted, run-down, baby-brained state, I missed a step and took quite the tumble. Instinct sent my arms flying out to catch the hand rail. Oh, I caught it all right. I caught it so freaking hard that I dislocated my shoulder.

Of course, I didn't realize it at the time. I picked myself up and started to walk back to my desk. I thought I saw a few stars, maybe a few Tweety birds, but I pushed them to the back of my mind. I had work to do. I couldn't afford to get behind!

"Umm, Vicki?" a co-worker asked as I passed her desk. "Are you O.K.? Why don't you sit down?"

I complied, and then dared to look at my shoulder. I pulled the neckline of my shirt to reveal my bone protruding at a nauseating angle.

Needless to say, I slowed down after that. For the two weeks my arm was in a sling, I didn't have a choice. Caring for two kids with one arm is no easy feat. It forces you to reevaluate your priorities and focus on only the most important tasks.

The house got messy. I showered every other day. I let Papa change all the diapers (I was *really* bummed about that one, let me tell you.)

Then, bit by bit, things started to get better. My shoulder healed. A third round of antibiotics finally knocked out my bronchitis. I could see the bottom of my to-do list, even though it was still miles long.

The universe had almost succeeded in taking me down, but I was fighting back. I would show the world once again that I could do it all!

Yeah right.

The pinnacle of this foolishness came one chilly day in December, when I had an appointment for a *visite médicale*. These medical visits are supposed to take place before you begin work—before your official start date if you're a new hire, or before you return after maternity/medical leave. I'd already been back to the post-maternity grind for more than two months, but in case you forgot, I live in France. My appointment date was practically early for French bureaucracy.

"*Bonjour, Madame*," the receptionist said. "The doctor will see you in a minute. In the meantime, would you be able to pee in a cup?"

Pee in a cup? *This* I could do. After two pregnancies and numerous check-ups, I was a pro.

The receptionist showed me to the restroom and set the empty cup next to the sink. "You can leave the cup here when you're finished."

Ah, a lovely bathroom all to myself! I thought. *No kids barging in and interrupting. This might actually be fun!*

I took off my coat and hung it on a hook. *Let's relax and enjoy ourselves here!* It'd been ages since I had this kind of privacy.

Then I blew the heck out of my nose. The bronchitis was on its way out, but was leaving a snotty path of destruction in its wake, which required frequent, lengthy nose-blowing sessions.

I spotted a poster with a tired-looking woman on it and read the message: "Get seven to eight hours of sleep at night or else you'll look like this." Umm, poster? Looking like that would be a step UP from my current state. That woman clearly didn't have two babies at home.

Finally, I used the toilet, then washed my hands. I looked in the mirror to check that I looked O.K.—O.K. was the best I could expect —then turned to grab my coat.

And that's when I saw it. The empty cup.

I'd been sent to the restroom with one mission: to pee in a cup. I'd been in there a total of two minutes, tops. And I had completely forgotten to PEE IN THE CUP.

What could I do? I didn't have the urge to go any more. I couldn't wait around until I had to go again. I would just have to leave my empty cup on the counter.

I briefly wondered if I should explain what happened to the receptionist. I envisioned the awkward conversation:

Me: So, I left an empty cup in the restroom. It's funny, really. I was in there and I just ... completely forgot to pee in it.

Receptionist: You forgot? You were in there two minutes. How could you forget? Maybe you don't know the right word in French. Are you sure you FORGOT?

Me: Oh yes, that's it. I know the word for 'forgot.' It's clearly the only thing I *haven't* forgotten.

The receptionist shakes her head and tsk-tsks.

No, better to keep my mouth shut. The urine sample was optional anyway. She could just think I'd changed my mind. I'd entered the stall and decided I didn't want to share my urine with a total stranger after all.

I sat in the waiting room, hoping the doctor would call me into her office before the receptionist discovered my embarrassingly empty cup. That was the first time in my life a cup of pee would have been the *less* embarrassing option.

Then realization dawned. Had my kids been there, I wouldn't have forgotten to pee in the stupid cup. I never would have been able to relax in the first place or blow my nose in peace. I would have peed in the cup, sang a song to calm my crying daughter, and blocked my son from unrolling the entire toilet paper roll—all in less than thirty seconds.

Peeing alone had been my downfall.

On the bright side, I wouldn't likely get another moment to urinate in private for a long time. I'd return to multi-tasking soon. I'd be back Officially on Top of Things.

VICKI LESAGE proves daily that raising two French kids isn't as easy as the hype lets on. In her three minutes of spare time per week, she writes, sips bubbly, and prepares for the impending zombie apocalypse. She lives in Paris with her French husband, rambunctious son, and charming daughter, all of whom mercifully don't laugh when she says "au revoir." She penned two books, Confessions of a Paris Party Girl *and* Confessions of a Paris Potty Trainer, *in between diaper changes and wine refills. She writes about the ups and downs of life in the City of Light at* VickiLesage.com.

Mom's Alone-Time Agenda
By Robyn Welling
Hollow Tree Ventures

Once upon a time, I found myself in the house. Alone.

If that sounds like the beginning of a fairy tale, there's a reason: it's because I'm a mom. And most moms know that, ordinarily, alone time is about as close to becoming a reality as magical dragons and wish-granting genies, so it's no wonder I couldn't believe it at first.

I don't know how it happened. I can't say for sure where all the children were. All I know for certain is that at some point I had the urge to yell, "Keep it down in there!" and realized *no one was making noise.*

I went to investigate the silence, and after three steps I noticed I hadn't tripped on a tiny person dangling from my pant leg.

I couldn't remember the last time I'd told someone to quit asking for a cookie.

I was alone!

Actually, I knew what was going on—my husband had taken the kids with him to the store. However, by the time I came to grips with my aloneness and had begun to celebrate, they were already back; and I couldn't help but feel I'd wasted my precious Me Time in a semi-catatonic, slack-jawed state of disbelief. There were so many things I could have done—what a wasted opportunity!

I vowed never to let that happen again.

Next time everyone's out of the house, I'm determined to get the most out of every single second. How? By planning ahead.

Now, some people might be tempted to use this time for a shower or some such responsible nonsense, which is a common rookie mistake. Sure, it's nice to have the bathroom to yourself and rinse all the shampoo out of your hair—maybe even use conditioner! But think about it: Mom's Alone Time is for stuff *you* want to do. Once they're home, they won't mind you taking a shower eventually (if you wait long enough, they might even *beg* you to take one), but you can bet nobody's ever going to beg you to dance around the house in your underwear while listening to old Prince albums and singing passionately into a hair brush.

I Still Just Want to Pee Alone

Or whatever you do when you're alone—no judgment here.

I'm just saying, we have to make the most of it.

So, as soon as the door ~~slams behind~~ gently clicks shut on the heels of my husband and the brood the next time they go out, here's my plan of action:

1. Five minutes of grateful weeping—because, hey, I'm only human.
2. Pee with the bathroom door open. Bask in the glorious knowledge that no one will come in asking me to settle an argument or braid their hair while I do.
3. Boldly eat seventeen cookies in the middle of the kitchen without fear of sharing.
4. Clean cookie crumbs off the kitchen floor—because fun is fun, but I don't want to get ants.
5. Down on the floor, notice some old chunks of dried up cereal bar and petrified fruit snacks under the edge of the cabinets. Reluctantly acknowledge that I should sweep those up before the baby finds them and decides they might still be delicious.
6. There, that's better. While the vacuum's out, might as well sweep the living room ...
7. Gah, the couch looks like it's made entirely out of solid cat fur! I'll just hook up the attachment and vacuum the cushions. Might as well get between them, too ...
8. *What the hell is that godawful noise?!?* A Sasquatch gargling chainsaws? A thousand motorcycles in a blender? A bowling ball hurricane? Oh, no, I see—a couple Legos just got sucked into the vacuum hose. Because OF COURSE THERE ARE LEGOS IN THE COUCH. Where else would they be?
9. Try to ignore the new vacuum noise until I smell something like rubbery burning electronics. Unplug the vacuum, remove the canister and fish through the guts of it to retrieve the stupid Legos.
10. Reassemble the vacuum. Note that there's now a thin coating of dusty vacuum filth on everything within a twelve-foot radius. Take the canister, containing the discarded chunks of food and enough fur

to make a new cat, into the kitchen to empty it. Trip on the vacuum-cord and spill the canister onto the kitchen floor.   Around this time, my husband will be back with the kids. Both the house and myself will be even dirtier than when they left. The kids will have overheard the seven or eight obscenities I yelled as I face-planted onto the kitchen floor. My husband will need me to take the baby, since I'm "all rested" and he's been wrangling the kids on his own this whole time. Within seconds, one of the kids will see the cookie package I left on the counter.

"Ooooh, Mommy, can I have a cookie, too?"

Hmm, it seems my grand plan went off the rails somewhere shortly after the weeping, which is probably why the plan ends in weeping, too. Maybe we should try something more like this:

1. Forget the grateful weeping—screw those guys, you've *earned* this alone time!
2. Lock the door before they've pulled all the way out of the driveway.
3. Boldly eat *all* the cookies (over the sink so there are no crumbs to clean up). Wrap the cookie package in several lay-ers of oil-soaked rags and burn it so the kids will never find the evidence.
4. Check to make sure the door is still locked. Can't be too careful.
5. Do your version of dancing around in your underwear while lis-tening to old Prince albums and singing passionately into a hair brush. Yes, even if your version of a great time means taking an unin-terrupted shower and rinsing all the shampoo out of your hair—I was lying about them letting you take one later, anyway.

I Still Just Want to Pee Alone

ROBYN WELLING is the freelance writer, humorist and editor behind <u>Hollow Tree Ventures</u>, where she isn't afraid to embarrass herself—and frequently does. She's been named a Must-Follow Humor Blog and co-authored three best-selling humor anthologies, yet her kids still don't think she's funny. Her goals include becoming independently wealthy, followed by world domination and getting her children to clean their rooms. Until then, she'll just fold laundry and write about the shortcuts she takes on her journey to becoming a somewhat passable wife, mother and human being; if history is any guide, she'll miss the mark entirely. You can find her avoiding responsibility on <u>Facebook</u>, <u>Twitter</u> and <u>Pinterest</u>.

And Then God Laughed
By Suzanne Fleet
Toulouse and Tonic

Growing up with three sisters alone in the house much of the time while my parents worked, my memories mainly consist of two things. 1. Watching soap operas after school while licking the cheese coating off each individual Dorito and 2. Hysterical fights involving high-pitched screaming, batons, fingernails and all three of our voices simultaneously telling on each other from a different extension of our landline phone to my poor mother while she tried to work.

My sisters and I fought a lot over the course of fifteen years. We fought over Barbie dolls, we fought about chores, we fought because one of us was looking at the other. I thought our battles were constant, outsize, and full of enough drama to earn each of us a special category Oscar statuette. I also imagined that my parents could have fixed all of the strife by being a little bit more like Mr. and Mrs. Brady. But mostly I knew that when I grew up, my household would be different.

And then God laughed. And gave me boys.

They have one simple requirement in order to fight with each other and that is just to be in the same place. God help us when they acquire cell phones.

Asher and Meyer are smallish boys right now—seven and three—with a large age gap between them that I was foolish enough to think would cushion the sibling rivalry. In my mind, one would be into Minecraft while the other was into Elmo. Clear age-appropriate boundaries would keep things nice and peaceful around our household.

"Hahahahaha! Oh my Me, I can even … " I heard God up there gasping, laughing his holy ass off.

Things on the sibling rivalry front were not too bad for the first few months. Asher was newly five, and had adapted pretty well to having an immobile baby brother around. "Oh isn't he cute? Can we put him to bed now?"

But then Meyer began to sit up—and Gabe and I were forever putting them next to each other for photos and because OMG

I Still Just Want to Pee Alone

BROTHERS! The heartening thing was that Asher was actually pretty gentle with his five-month-old baby brother. The baby, on the other hand, turned out to be a professional wrestling prodigy. As soon as he was next to Asher, Meyer would turn towards him with a mischievous grin on his face—then stretch his chubby arms out wide, push off with his legs and booty and just tackle him, laughing with glee. I have a vivid memory of attempting a photo of them side by side at Christmastime and the vision of baby Santa tackling an overgrown elf repeatedly while I ran back and forth from them to the camera still makes me dissolve into giggle fits. Because that was back when it was still funny.

When Meyer began to crawl, they fought because he was drooling on all of Asher's things. As soon his brother started walking, Asher requested help making a sign for his bedroom door that said, "No babies allowed!!!!" then covered every leftover inch of space with disturbingly angry frowny faces.

But the milestone that spelled the permanent end of even respites of peace and quiet was when Meyer learned to talk.

At three, he's not only developed an extensive contest-based vocabulary of bigger, faster, better, stronger, but also a screeching "NOOOOOOOOOOOOOOOO!" that would make no gift more desirable than a decent pair of noise canceling headphones.

There is nothing they won't fight about.

Here's a short list:

Who will sit next to me.

Who can pound themselves in the head harder.

Who will grow bigger.

Who ate the most chicken nuggets.

Whether the dog's favorite color is green or dark blue.

Who likes Batman.

Who licked the other first.

What show to watch.

Who cannonballed off the couch better.

Who was breathing louder.

Who runs faster.

Who is old enough to play with Legos.
Who can stay up later.
Who's going first.
Who farted.
Who ate the last banana.
Whose muscles are bigger.
Video game interference.
Who will let the dog out.
Who will let the dog in.
Who started it.
Who said "potty talk" and
GIVETHATBACKIWASPLAYINGWITHTHAT!
And that was just the last half hour.

They even fight for airspace. If one of them starts talking, the other talks louder—each one increasing the volume in turn until my eardrums have been pounded with so much noise, I begin to feel like I've just come from a twenty-four hour Metallica concert. It's not uncommon for them to run out of things to say and just decide to yell "Lalalalalalalala" at the top of their lungs in order to drown the other one out.

And most foreign of all to me is the physical fighting. They seem compelled to lock their bodies together in combat, never loosening a grip until one or both of them is sobbing uncontrollably. They've shown me that even a peaceable activity like making Valentines can escalate into a death match in a few seconds flat.

I look for answers in other families with boys, both young and grown. "Is it normal for them to fight this much?" I ask brothers and mothers.

The unequivocal answer is always, "God, yes."

They almost invariably move on to stories that contain phrases like butcher knife, concussion, broken arm, fire extinguishers, scars, mud wrestling, and BB guns—and then I tell them I have to go—I've pretty much got all I can handle right now.

To which someone often replies, "God never gives you more than you can handle."

I Still Just Want to Pee Alone

And then I hear him up there laughing so hard he can't breathe, pounding on Heaven's floor, making a sound like thunder. But I can't hear it because my boys are fighting with each other again.

Suzanne Fleet is the writer and humorist behind the award-winning blog, <u>Toulouse & Tonic</u>, and mom to two stinky boys, who together with her good-natured husband, give her loads of hilarious writing material. Suzanne is one of PopSugar's Top 25 Funny Moms and a contributor to Today.com and Huffington Post as well as a proud co-author of the best-selling books *I Just Want To Pee Alone, I Just Want To Be Alone* and *You Have Lipstick on Your Teeth*. She'll soon be releasing her own book of essays about motherhood and marriage.

Post-Kid Me Wishes Pre-Kid Me
Would Kiss Post-Kid Me's Tender Behind
By Meredith Bland
Pile of Babies

There's a great joke that goes, "I was the perfect mom before I had kids."

From time to time, mothers come across people who don't have children, but who still have all the answers about what they should or should not be doing with their child. This advice is typically met with false appreciation followed by sarcastic laughter with their mom friends the next day. It's not that those non-moms are *trying* to be obnoxious, and it's not that those moms are *trying* to be mean. It's just that unless you've had to care for a child twenty-four hours a day, seven days a week, then you might want to keep your opinions to yourself because you ain't about that life.

I can say this because not only have I been on the receiving end of those helpful comments ("Wow. Your baby must be freezing cold. Where are her socks?") and because I was once that childless woman who looked at other mothers and thought to myself, "When I have kids, I'll do it better."

I know. It's hilarious. I look back at some of the plans I had for motherhood, and I can't believe I was ever so naïve and obnoxious. Come along with me as I take you to seven years ago, back to when I was a childless woman with high ideals and a fantastic ass. I'm going to share with you some of the honest-to-God things I thought about parenting before I had my own kids and realized what an utter asshole I was.

"Two-year-olds need to learn patience."

One day, my husband and I went out for lunch with my in-laws, my sister-in-law, and my then two-year-old niece. We ordered our food, and my sister-in-law said to the waiter, "If you could bring hers [meaning my niece's] out first, that'd be great." And Lord, let me tell you, I was appalled. Appalled, I say! On the drive home, I remember saying to my husband, "How is she going to learn to wait if she gets her meals before everybody else? She should learn to wait like the rest of us."

See what I mean? I was such a dick.

That kid was two. In a restaurant. Clearly, I had no idea what I was talking about. These days when I take my twins out to eat, I only go to restaurants that are a) loud and b) tend to bring your food within ten minutes of ordering. And yes, if you can bring my kids meals as soon as they're ready, I would love it.

"I'll only use wooden toys, never plastic."

This one I held on to through my pregnancy. My mother would show me toys that she wanted to buy for the babies, and I would say, "Hmm. I don't know. That's an awful lot of plastic. I want to avoid as many plastic toys as I can and try to stick with ones only made of wood." I think my mother said something like, "Ha! Aha ha ha ha ha ha!" And today, looking back, I admire her restraint. What the hell was I thinking? I'm not a hard-core environmentalist. I don't live in the woods. I was having twins for God's sake. By the time my kids were six-months-old you had to vault over the walker, dodge the Exersaucer, limbo under the Jumparoo, and then do an army crawl across the activity mat just to get from the front door to the bedroom.

Only wooden toys. For the love of Pete …

"I'll be able to handle the sleep deprivation. After all, I pulled all-nighters in college."

I'll give you a moment to collect yourself.

It's true. I actually thought that the sleep deprivation that comes with a baby would be no worse than studying for my economics final. Part of this is understandable because unless you've experienced what it's like to go on that little sleep you can't even begin to imagine what it's really like. So, I guess I'm saying that it's only new moms and Navy Seals that really get it.

I have a sister who's a doctor, and she tried to convince me that the lack of sleep you get when you have a baby is like the lack of sleep you get when you are going through your medical residency. And then I laughed and laughed. No offense to any doctors out there because y'all are tougher than I am by a mile, but having a baby is only like residency if residency lasts all day every day and doesn't end for years. I was so insane by the time my kids were three-months-old, that I was hallucinating and having to hold my head up with my hands to stay awake. I wasn't eating because I would look at the kitchen and say, "Man, I'm hungry. I should get up, walk over to the fridge, get out the ham and the bread and the mayo, open them up and oh fuck it I'd rather starve sitting down."

The exhaustion that comes with having a baby is no joke, and I am thankful that this is one pre-child opinion that I did keep to myself. I feel pretty sure that if I had said that out loud in front of another parent they would never stop asking me if I were kidding. I'm talking phone calls in the middle of the night five years later from someone saying, "Hey, remember when you said that thing about sleep deprivation not being a big deal ... that was a joke right? Yeah, I'm sorry, it's just that extra special kind of stupid that still haunts me."

"Why did they have kids if they don't want to hang out with them?"

Oh, yeah. There's the kicker. I was one of those self-righteous schmucks who could not for the life of me understand why parents would want to be away from their kids or how they could make jokes about how awful parenting could be. I mean, parenting is giggles and cotton and sunlight streaming through the windows of clean rooms that are inexplicably filled with white furniture, right?

No.

Parenting is hard. In fact, it's the hardest thing I've ever done. And for large parts of the day, parenting is not rewarding; it's stressful, infuriating, boring, and painful. But despite all of that, my children are the best part of my life and my reason for being. And that's how I could ask dumb questions like, "Why did she have kids if she doesn't want to spend time with them?" Because I didn't understand

163

what truly unconditional love was until I had my kids. It's being yelled at and shit on and made to feel worse than you ever have in your life, and still, at the end of the day, saying with tears in your eyes, "I love you more than anything in the universe. I am so lucky to be your mommy. Now please, just fucking go to sleep."

MEREDITH BLAND is a freelance writer whose work has appeared in Brain, Mother; Blogher; Scary Mommy; Mamapedia; and Time. A former staff writer at Mommyish, Meredith enjoys writing a whole lot of nonsense on her blog, Pile of Babies.

Hammers and Swords, Oh My!
By Sarah Cottrell
Housewife Plus

I always knew that once I became a mother there would be some degree of repressing my former childless self. The music I once adored would become highly offensive around my kids. I mean, really, have you ever listened to Liz Phair or Jay Z? The food I once drooled over would be replaced by bright orange bite sized nuggets of whatever it is that kids eat. Goodbye, sushi. Hello, mac and cheese. Bathroom time would no longer be a private affair but more like a semi-public theater of the absurd much in the same way that surgery rooms were during the turn of the twentieth century.

Goodbye, dignity. Hello, motherhood.

I was OK with much of that when I signed up for this mothering business. Heck, in some ways I even reveled in the martyring of myself in just how overwhelming my new duties were. My friends and I would have online chats about who was the most tired, the most irritated, the most whatever. It was a like a pissing contest for new moms.

But then one day everything changed. My children, both boys, one a toddler and the other a preschooler, had discovered swords. And ninjas. And dragon slayers. They pretty much discovered that they could be either a hero or a villain and with that revelation everything in my house was suddenly up for grabs as loot, weaponry, or on a hit list to go missing or broken.

Ah, motherhood. No longer was it fun to complain about how tired I was. Now it was out and out survival of wits. The winner would have to have endurance, stamina, and sugar in mass quantities in order to win. It was a tight race between my kids and I as to who would be the last exhausted person standing. Motherhood was turning out to be a bitch.

My mani-pedi bag that holds my files, pumice stones, polishes, and cuticle sticks went missing. My knitting needles went missing. Every single wooden spoon in my kitchen went missing. My husband and I found ourselves tossing our oldest son's room at least once a week in search of something that at one time seemed innocuous but now was a potential hazard, like my pencil sharpener shaped like a bi-plane.

Every time we had to talk to our son about safety we would inevitably leave the conversation wanting to shove wads of cotton in our ears. Kids are so damn stubborn.

Me: Sweetie, you can't use my knitting needles as swords, it just isn't safe!

Husband: Wow, you really did a good job making it look like a real swashbuckling sword by deflating that plastic ball and poking it with the knitting needle. Geesh ... inventive!

Me: Oh, my God, Honey ... are you serious?!

Husband: What? I mean, c'mon, it is pretty damn creative!

Me: Ok, listen, knitting needles and everything else sharp and pokey are just off limits. Got it, kiddo?

Kid: MMMMOOOOMMMMM!!!! YOU ARE THE WORST EVERRRRRRRRR!

Me: Thanks, Honey. He thinks I'm the jerk now."

Kid: That's it! I'm going to live with Grammy! She isn't mean! She lets me have swords! She gives me cake! She lets me do anything I want to do! And I HATE YOU!

After a few weeks of this we started to notice that our oldest son was getting bored and tired from all the mom and dad interventions on his fun time. He found other things to distract himself with. Namely, drawing on the walls with markers.

Meanwhile, our youngest son who was a newly minted toddler was keenly aware of *everything* that was going on around him. He was copying his big brother but was getting away with murder because, well, he was just so stupidly cute about everything. My husband and I clearly had "sucker" tattooed on our dumb parenting faces and the little one was eating this up.

The climax of this newly refined behavior came one day when I walked into the bathroom and found my toddler son whacking his wooden play bench with what I can only imagine was what he must have thought was the coolest hammer he had ever encountered.

My jaw nearly hit the damn floor.

The child was using my Hitachi vibrator as a hammer to play Whack-A-Mole with his Melissa and Doug Deluxe Pound-A-Peg game.

What. The. Ever. Loving. Fuck?

Now, this is not just any vibrator. This is known as the Cadillac of vibrators and cost damn near as much. The wand is roughly a foot long with a pivoting neck attached to a tennis ball-sized white rubber head. There are only two settings, high and low. Let me just tell you that after nearly fifteen years with my Hitachi, I have not once yet been able to dare myself to go to the high setting. The low setting is about as effective as a jackhammer. And believe me. It. Does. The. Job. Well.

So. Back to the bathroom. The toddler is hammering his primary colored wooden pegs with an eighty dollar vibrator that has seen me through every phase of my marriage and motherhood. I was one part amused (I mean come on, I'm telling you this story and you must be laughing by now, right?) and all the other parts totally freaking horrified!

In the span of maybe four seconds the following thoughts flew through my head faster than the speed of light:

Holy mother of fucking what the ack! Gah!

Oh no! Oh, crap! This CANNOT be happening. Oh, my … My husband will never let me live this down. OH MY GOD, DID HE JUST DENT THE CADILLAC?!?!?!OH FUCK! HE DID—Wait, nope, he totally didn't. Well, this will be a shining moment in his future therapy sessions.

Without making even an iota of fuss I simply walked over, quickly took the vibrator out of his toddler mitts, handed him a sippy cup and started babbling to him about snack time and Curious George.

Exhale … sigh of relief … the kid hardly noticed…

Later that night when my husband came home from work I had to fess up to him that our smallest child found my vibrator and was using it as a hammer to whack his pegs with. After what amounted to a lot of laughing at my expense and some finger pointing we had to add items of the dirty drawer variety to the seemingly unending list of household junk that needed to be banned because the kids found an inventive way to use them as weapons.

SARAH COTTRELL is a stay-at-home-mom in rural Maine. In 2012 she earned her MFA and immediately shoved it in the back of a closet where appliances go to die. When she is not chasing her kids or cleaning her house, Sarah writes a blog at the Bangor Daily News *called Housewife Plus. Her irreverent humor has been featured on a laundry list of parenting sites including Scary Mommy and The Huffington Post where she is a regular contributor.*

The Last Time We Did One, Two, Three
By Michelle Poston Combs
Rubber Shoes in Hell

When you have a child, especially the first one, you feel like they will be babies for a life time. They fit in the crook of your arm where they stay for hours as you watch them yawn and stretch and smile. Even though the doctor tells you they aren't *really* smiling, you know they are.

Then you blink.

They are out of diapers, into disposable underwear that are really just annoying diapers, and you carry them on your hip. These are the days you are likely to end up with a bank's lime lollipop stuck in your hair.

Then you blink.

By the time his hair loses the baby fineness, he will graduate to your shoulders and it's good, although, you do spend a lot of time just waiting to get peed on.

Then you blink and he slides down your back and wraps his legs around your waist.

I guess the way to stop these changes from happening is to just stop blinking.

Except not blinking doesn't work. It makes no difference if you rail against them growing up. Crying about your children changing doesn't stop the changes from happening. Fearing the future doesn't keep the future at bay. Whether you blink or not, one day your child will be too big to pick up.

I could carry my older son, Zach, until he was somewhere between nine and ten years old. By then, he was half my size, but we could still swing it. He would put his arm around my neck and we would both bob at the knees and count to three. On three, he would jump onto my hip and I would wrap my arm around his waist.

Then one day I noticed, I really noticed, that my baby boy, the one that I thought would be a baby forever, was eye to eye with me. He was eleven years old and not the skinny kid he used to be. By age eleven, he probably weighed about the same as the average supermodel. I don't think I could carry a supermodel, either. I'm short, so if for no other reason, it would be because their long supermodel legs were dragging the ground.

When I realized that my son was too big to carry, I tried to remember the last time we did one, two, three.

We were probably walking through the parking lot of our apartment complex in Wichita. There was a grocery store next door to our apartment complex, so walking the length of the parking lot was common. He was probably lagging behind and dragging his feet and I was probably nagging at him to cut it out. Did he think shoes were free? They weren't cheap and he'd be needing new ones soon enough. Then I was probably nagging him about the state of his bedroom and where he left his bike. Once I got a good nag going, it was hard to stop.

He probably caught up with me and said "Mom, let's do one, two, three." I'm sure I was tired, but I said okay. After he was on my hip, I probably staggered along for ten or twelve steps before putting him down saying "You're ten now. You are getting too big for this." Then he probably dropped back and lagged behind the rest of the way home. That is probably how it went the last time I carried my son.

But I'm not sure. I don't remember at all what happened the last time.

I wish so bad that I could remember the last time I carried him. We think these commonplace events will never end. You do the same things over and over. How many times did you wash that pacifier off in the sink? There was a last time. Honestly, it was probably at least a month or two before you actually took the pacifier away. We go from boiling them to picking pet hair off them pretty quick. Or was that just me?

Since I don't remember the last time I carried my son, I am going to make up my own memory. I get to do that.

This is what happened the last time I carried my son, Zachary:

The heat from the August sun reflected from the asphalt as Zach and I walked across the parking lot to our apartment from the grocery store. We had gone to the grocery to eat humongous cinnamon rolls with extra icing. I let Zach get two cartons of chocolate milk, instead of one. He had a chocolate mustache that mixed with the sweat on his upper lip.

Our moving truck was packed and ready to go. We were leaving Wichita and moving back to Kentucky. My stomach hurt because Zach's baby brother was busy growing there, even though none of us knew that yet. Zach's stomach hurt because I shouldn't have let him have that second chocolate milk.

"Mommy, let's do one, two, three."

"Sure, Baby."

He put his arm around my neck. We bobbed at the knees and counted down. Then there he was, on my hip. We were eye to eye and his hair smelled of sunshine. He rested his head against mine and I sailed through the parking lot with nary a stagger. I had the strength of ten Grinches that afternoon. We walked past the moving van and I floated up the stairs to our second floor apartment without having to hold the rail. I had both of my boys with me and they weighed nothing at all.

I carried Zach inside the apartment and held him against me until he started to squirm to be let down. "You can put me down now, Mom."

I put him down and it was then that I could feel his weight.

He smiled a chocolate smile and said "I love you, Mommy."

I stroked his cheek and told him I loved him, too.

That is how it happened. That was the last time we did one, two, three. I didn't complain about how heavy he was getting. I didn't say that I wouldn't be able to carry him much longer because he was getting too old for such things. I just carried my son.

I knew it was the last time that I would carry him, but I wasn't sad. I knew that he was growing up strong and good and I had finished my job of carrying him. I knew it was time that he carried himself.

I wasn't sad because I remembered to remember the last time we did one, two, three.

I Still Just Want to Pee Alone

A few years after the last time I carried my older son, I watched him carry his brother, Joey. I wanted to tell Zach to remember those times. Remember how carrying your brother feels because the number of times is finite and it's a much smaller number than you think.

I didn't, though. I just let him carry his brother without giving him the weight of the knowledge that one day it would end. One day his brother would be too big to carry.

Before Joey was out of diapers, Zach's voice changed. He sauntered instead of skipped. He grew up and I grew older.

But I can still remember the last time I carried my son.

No one can tell me that it happened any other way.

MICHELLE POSTON COMBS lives with her husband and her son. She is heading toward an empty nest which she finds terrifying and exhilarating.

Her blog, Rubber Shoes In Hell, is where she covers topics ranging from awkward conversations to learning how to overcome being an adult child of a narcissist.

Today and Tomorrow
By Beth Caldwell
The Cult of Perfect Motherhood

Often when I'm spending time with my kids, I think about how they will remember that moment when they're grown. I never spent much time imagining their future before I found the lump that turned out to be metastatic breast cancer, but these days, I think about it a lot.

The kids know I have cancer, and they know sometimes I feel like shit and I need more breaks and more rest than I used to. But at ages seven and three, they're small enough that they can't fully understand the ramifications of my diagnosis. Metastatic breast cancer is always fatal—eventually. But at this point in my disease progression, it's impossible for my husband and I to be having conversations about my prognosis with kids of their cognitive ability. If we said "cancer is going to kill Mommy someday," they'd be spending all their time worrying if someday is tomorrow, when hopefully it's five or ten or twenty years from now.

Instead, we talk about how Mommy is living with cancer today. We talk about where the tumors are, and we talk about the testing and the chemo and the radiation. And they check out my mastectomy scar and they meet my oncologist and they tell me my hair is growing back gray. The reality of my treatment and the changes to my body are part of their world now, and *now* is where kids function.

It puts me outside my comfort zone to *not* talk to them about my prognosis, though. I'm a firm believer in being straight with your kids about even the most uncomfortable of topics. When my son was almost six and he asked me how babies are created, I calmly explained the mechanics of sex to him, and it didn't make either of us uncomfortable at all. We often discuss issues of racism and war and drugs and all kinds of things that make other parents say, "Let's talk about that when you're older." It's just how I roll. I'm an open book with my kids.

Except, I can't be an open book with them about the reality that I'm going to die of cancer someday.

And even though I know it's right for us not to discuss it, I sometimes feel almost like I'm lying to them, because prognosis is always on my mind. In every moment with them, in every interaction, I'm thinking about how long I have with them, wondering whether I have two more Christmases or twenty, if I will be there to make pancakes with them on a rainy Sunday morning when they're twelve years old. I look at them and feel a deep and painful longing for that future we can't discuss, because it's too speculative, and too scary, and not where they live. And maybe not where I will live either.

So I set that longing aside, and I put on a mask, a mask that one day I'll have to take off for them, when they're old enough to understand, or when I'm too sick to keep the mask on anymore. And I joke and laugh with them and try my best to make sure that when I'm gone, there's no doubt in their minds that I loved them, and also that I knew they loved me too, so that they have no reason to feel guilt or regret about our relationship.

In many ways, I'm no longer like other parents, because of my illness. But in putting on that mask for the kids and not showing them the pain I feel when I think about their future without me, in doing what's best for them even though it's hard for me, I can be like every other parent in the world. As uncomfortable as it is for me, wearing that mask is something I can do that makes me feel like a normal mom. In the times when I can't do the things I used to do as a parent, I can still put on my brave face and listen to them tell a joke or talk to me about their day and hug them and laugh and smile and do anything—anything—to make it so that when they look back on that moment, they'll know that they brought me joy, and that I loved them.

This is what all parents want for our children—for them to know they are loved, and that they are important to us. And in my darkest moments, I take comfort in knowing that despite everything, I can help them make memories today that will travel with them into the future I have lost.

BETH CALDWELL is a former civil rights attorney and mom of two. She was diagnosed with metastatic breast cancer in the spring of 2014.

A Good Parent Finds Their Child's Weakness and Then Exploits the Hell Out of It
By Jen Mann
People I Want to Punch in the Throat

When I was a new mother, it drove me crazy when mothers of older children would gaze longingly at my tantruming toddler thrashing around on the floor of Panera and say "Enjoy this time when they're little, it goes so fast."

It took all my self-restraint to keep from saying, "You can have her."

However, now that my kids are ten and eight, I'm starting to understand what those moms were talking about. If I start thinking about the fact that my son is over half way through his time with us and will leave for college in eight years, I'll start crying.

Quick. Somebody hand me a baby to huff—preferably one with a poopy diaper. It's the only cure for the feels that I'm feeling.

Whoa! That was a close one. Now, let me be clear! I'm not saying I want another baby. No, no, no, no, *no*! I'm fully basking in the light at the end of the tunnel and I'm ninety-eight percent certain that the light isn't from an approaching train. I love the fact that everyone can wipe their own butt now, tie their own shoes, sort of make breakfast for themselves, read quietly, or turn on the television to entertain themselves all while I catch a few more zzzzs on Saturday morning. I'm just saying those wise mothers of middle schoolers were right. It seems like just yesterday my son was trying to lovingly smother his baby sister with a Ziploc bag.

Hey, it happens, people. Watch out! True story, when Adolpha was six weeks old, we took her to the pediatrician for her check up. Everything looked great. Then he looked over at two-year-old Gomer. He asked how Gomer was getting along with Adolpha. "He loves her to pieces," I replied.

"Right. Good," he said. "Now, listen, besides SIDS and accidentally rolling off of things, that right there"—he pointed to Gomer—"is the the number one baby killer in your house. He doesn't know his own strength, he has no concept of what he's doing. He could literally love her to death. Suffocate her, crush her, what have you. *Never* leave them in a room alone together."

Yikes! At the time I thought my doctor was a little intense and I blew him off. It was about about a month or so later when I left Gomer and Adolpha alone in the playroom for a moment while I tried to pee in peace that I heard Gomer say, "Oooh, pretty hat, Adolpha."

I couldn't think of any hats we had in the playroom, what was Gomer doing? I clenched mid-stream, frantically wiped, and ran out of the bathroom with my pants around my ankles to find Gomer placing a large Ziploc bag we used to hold puzzle pieces over Adolpha's head. It was too big to sit around her head like a hat and it kept slipping down over her eyes and nose while both of my children laughed. "OH. MY. GOD!" I screamed, diving across the room and ripping the bag off of her head. "What are you doing, Gomer?"

Gomer immediately started crying and begging for forgiveness. He wasn't sure what he'd done wrong exactly, but he knew I was mad or upset and he'd better start showing some remorse and making it all better pronto. At the time I didn't realize that that was Gomer's personality. I always assumed it was my superior parenting that made Gomer such a good kid. Gomer was the kid you could give The Look to from about six months on. He would crawl up to an outlet and I'd warn him, "Goooomer." He'd smile and shake his head and crawl away. If I told him to clean up his toys, he did so without any fuss. If I said it was bedtime, he climbed into his bed and waited for me. He ate his vegetables, he rarely cried, he never threw toys, or hit anyone. I was a parenting genius. Just ask me, I would have told you.

Then Adolpha arrived. She was just as beautiful, just as pink, and just as healthy as Gomer. She looked just like him. She was even born on his second birthday. I was sure that once I unleashed my patent-pending brand of awesome parenting on her, she'd fall into line just like Gomer.

Right off the bat, Adolpha gave us clues that she was not the same kind of baby as Gomer. She refused to be held and cried all the time. The only person that could make her happy was Gomer and even then it was only when he did things like put Ziploc bags over head. As much as she loved Gomer, she also hated him. She hated how much older he was and how he could do super cool things like get food into his mouth on the first try and walk. When she'd become frustrated, she would crawl over to Gomer and stand up on her knees to reach him. He'd think she was coming in for a sweet hug and instead she'd haul off and slap him across the face and then she'd crawl away and hide while the Hubs and I tried to console Gomer. He always reminded me of Nancy Kerrigan, holding his red face and screaming, "*Why? Why me, Mama?*"

I wanted to say, I don't know, Gomer. I don't know. Also, you're not very bright, son. Why haven't you yet figured out that you're going to get the crap beat out of you? You can run—she can't—run the next time she's coming your way, Gomer.

We were stymied by Adolpha. My fabulous parenting skills weren't working on her! She cared about no one and nothing. We'd always been the type of discipliners (that's a word, right?) who took away things. Legos, Matchbox cars, screen time. Just the mere threat of the removal of these items from Gomer's life kept him on the straight and narrow.

Adolpha? Not so much. The first time she hit Gomer, we took all of her toys and put them in time out and gave her the whole, "We don't hit, Gomer. We love Gomer" speech. She just stared at us with soulless eyes and I swear she checked her nails for dirt. "Now, because you hurt Gomer—who you love—all of your dolls and puzzles will be off limits for one day," I said to her.

She yawned, shrugged her shoulders, and scampered off.

Two days went by before I even remembered her toys. I felt terrible. "Adolpha! Mommy forgot to give you back your toys yesterday," I said to her. "Didn't you miss them?"

She shrugged her shoulders again. I swear, she was the only fourteen-month-old kid I knew of who could already roll her eyes and shrug her shoulders.

I got down her bucket of dolls and she didn't even look at them. Instead, she went over to Gomer, smiled sweetly at him, hauled back her arm, and whacked him across the face.

"ADOLPHA!" We both screamed.

She turned and stared at me with no emotion.

Holy shit, I thought. *I'm raising a sociopath!*

I yelled for the Hubs to come help. He came in and quickly assessed the situation. "That's it!" he said, shaking his head. "It's time to spank her, Jen. She needs a good spanking."

"No!" I intervened. The Hubs and I had both been raised by spankers. Not to the point that it was abusive or anything, but I've had a wooden spoon broken on my backside and I've felt the sting of a leather belt several times. I'm not saying it ruined my life or anything, but let's see … I write some pretty dark humor and I swear a lot. Coincidence?

When we first decided to have kids, the Hubs and I talked about spanking. We agreed that it really didn't do much in the way of changing our behavior when we were kids and it terrified us both. We decided that we'd ONLY spank if the kids were doing something dangerous like running out in traffic or messing around with knives and outlets.

At that point we'd been parents for a little over three years and we'd never had to spank our kids. Actually, that's not true. When Gomer was learning to walk, he would pull himself up on furniture and toddle around. One day—again while I was peeing!—I heard the ornaments on the Christmas tree in the living room jingling and clanking together. What the—? I clenched off the flow, wiped, and tripped over my pants to get to the living room just in time to see my twelve-foot tall tree leaning precariously over my baby who was trying to use the branches to pull himself up. It took all of my strength to keep that damn tree from tipping over on the both of us. By the time I got the tree righted and secured, I was shaking with fear and I grabbed Gomer and spanked his butt. "No, no, no!" I said with each hit.

I use the word hit, but really swat is a better word. I couldn't put my back into it and Gomer's enormous diaper protected him. He thought it was a game and laughed his ass off for the rest of the day while he trotted around the house, spanking his own butt and yelling, "No, no, no!"

I failed that day. It was a sign. I obviously couldn't put the power and fear that was necessary into a good spanking, so I shouldn't even try. It was the universe telling me not to spank my kids.

"No, Hubs," I begged him. "We agreed. No spanking. Besides, what's the message we're sending? Don't hit Gomer or else we'll hit you? How will she learn from that?"

"I don't know, but I'm sick of watching her beat up Gomer. We have to do something. If nothing else it will show Gomer that we're taking it seriously."

"Wait," I said. "Look." Adolpha was on the move again. She was crawling back over to Gomer. He was still sniffling a bit and holding his cheek.

"Adolpha," he cried. "you hurt me!"

"Sowwy, Goh!" she said.

"She apologized! Did you hear that?" I nudged the Hubs. "She's learning. She's . . ."

Adolpha picked up a DVD case lying on the floor near Gomer, inspected it carefully …

"Oh no! Move Gomer, she's going to—"

And then my precious pumpkin psychopath cracked Gomer across the face with the DVD case while she laughed maniacally.

"I've had it!" the Hubs roared.

The Hubs thrashed about in anger, feeling the need to beat the crap out something. Anything. And then he saw *him*.

PUPPY.

Puppy was a stuffed animal that Adolpha had recently become attached to. She'd been quite careful the first year of her life and didn't really glom onto to anything that we could take away and use as punishment, but we'd noticed that this dog was with her more and more lately. She'd made a fatal error. She'd developed an affinity for something and now we could use it like her own Achille's Heel.

The Hubs eyes lit up and he grabbed Puppy by the throat and held him up in the air.

"Looky what I have, Adolpha," the Hubs cackled. Apparently Adolpha, the psychopathic apple, didn't fall far from the Hubs' tree.

Adolpha stopped laughing and zeroed in on the Hubs, her eyes narrowed.

"Oh yeah, Adolpha. I have Puppy."

You could see Adolpha calculating her next move. Should she tantrum? Should she beg? She went with the Sad Kitty approach. Her glare softened, her eyes widened, and her lower lip popped out. "Puppy?" she whimpered.

She'd underestimated the Hubs. He was stronger than that. The Sad Kitty didn't even faze him. "What's the matter, Adolpha? Are you afraid I'm going to hurt him?" Hubs sneered.

Adolpha double downed on her Sad Kitty and worked up a single tear while she nodded her head and reached for Puppy.

The Hubs saw right through her ploy. He grunted and twisted Puppy's head all the way around.

Adolpha shuddered briefly and then her eyes went cold and she picked up the DVD case and held it out—threatening Gomer once more.

It was a stand off and the hell I was going to let my child be a hostage in the game Adolpha and the Hubs were playing.

"Gomer," I whispered. "Come here." He ran to me and out of Adolpha's reach.

"Mama?" Adolpha asked, turning her giant sweet Sad Kitty eyes on me.

My heart melted. I am a sucker for Sad Kitty. So rarely did Adolpha want me. She was a lone wolf who never wanted to be held or cuddled. Here she was reaching out to me. Asking for protection from her deranged father was going to decapitate her favorite stuffed animal. I couldn't deny her. "Yes, Adolpha. Come here too. I love you, Adolpha. Come to Mommy."

She crawled over and I picked her up. I sat her on my lap. She nuzzled my neck while I hugged her tightly. And then, while still nuzzling me and staring deep into my eyes, she reached over and slowly and deliberately snatched a handful of Gomer's glorious hair from his head. Gomer screamed.

"Sonofabitch" the Hubs yelled. "Argh!" And that's when he lost his mind and started beating the hell out of Puppy.

He punched him in the face, spanked his bottom, and rung his little stuffed neck.

All while Adolpha bellowed and thrashed around. She slid off my lap and threw herself on the floor. She banged her head against the couch cushions and acted as if the Hubs was hurting her instead of Puppy.

Gomer and I sat silently watching the spectacle. We were afraid to get too close for fear we'd become a victim of their tirades. After a five minute beat down, both the Hubs and Adolpha were exhausted.

"Are you ready … to … behave … Adolpha?" The Hubs gasped, trying to catch his breath. Beating up stuffed animals is hard work for middle-aged men who never work out.

Adolpha wiped her tears and nodded.

"Are you all done hitting Gomer?"

"No hit Puppy!" she cried.

"Well, every time you hit Gomer, I'll hit Puppy." The Hubs handed Puppy to Adolpha and she loved on that stuffed animal more than I'd ever seen her love on a live person.

The Hubs and I left the room. "What were you thinking?" I hissed.

"I wasn't," he said. "I was desperate."

"Well, it worked," I agreed. "We need to remember this for the next time she's in trouble."

And that right there is how you figure out *your* parenting technique. A book isn't going to teach you that. You're going to need to *gut* it. You're going to need to trust your instincts and to try anything—no matter how crazy it might sound at the time. Beating the shit out of your kid's stuffed animal might not work for you, but you'll find something that will.

That day we found Adolpha's weakness and since then we've exploited it for as long as we could. To this day Puppy is still a well loved member of Adolpha's inner circle and nothing hurts her more than us hurting Puppy. Puppy is now eight years old and quite frail, so we have to handle him very carefully, because it's way too easy to permanently "injure" him. I can't afford the therapy bills I'd have if Adolpha saw us rip off Puppy's head—even if it was an accident.

JEN MANN is best known for her wildly popular and hysterical blog People I Want to Punch in the Throat. She has been described by many as Erma Bombeck—with f-bombs. Jen is known for her hilarious rants and observations on everything from parenting to gift giving to celebrity behavior to Elves on Shelves. Her blog received the 2014 Bloggie Award for Best Parenting Blog. Jen is the author of the New York Times *bestseller* People I Want to Punch in the Throat: Competitive Crafters, Drop-Off Despots, and Other Suburban Scourges *which was a 2014 Finalist for a Goodreads Reader's Choice Award.*

Jen is a married mother of two children whom she calls Gomer and Adolpha in her writings—she swears their real names are worse.

NOTES FROM THE EDITOR

Thank you for reading this book. We appreciate your support and we hope you enjoyed it. We hope you will tell a friend—or thirty about this book. Please do us a huge favor and leave us a review on Amazon and Goodreads. Of course we prefer 5-star, but we'll take what we can get. If you hated this book, you can skip the review. *Namaste.*

Every contributor to this book has more for you to read. Please check out their blogs and books.

OTHER BOOKS AVAILABLE

I Just Want to Pee Alone

I Just Want to Be Alone

I STILL Just Want to Pee Alone

People I Want to Punch in the Throat: Competitive Crafters, Drop Off Despots, and Other Suburban Scourges

Spending the Holidays with People I Want to Punch in the Throat: Yuletide Yahoos, Ho-Ho-Humblebraggers, and Other Seasonal Scourges